Crossing
the Threshold of
Eternity

What the Dying Can
Teach the Living

ROBERT L. WISE

Guideposts
New York, New York

This Guideposts edition has been published by special arrangement with Gospel Light.

Published in association with the literary agency of WordServe Literary Group, Ltd., 10152 South Knoll Circle, Highlands Ranch, CO 80130.

The Library of Congress has cataloged the Regal Books edition as follows:

Library of Congress Cataloging-in-Publication Data
Wise, Robert L.
  Crossing the threshold of eternity : what the dying can teach the living / Robert L. Wise.
    p. cm.
  ISBN 978-0-8307-4370-4 (hard cover)
  1. Death—Religious aspects—Christianity. I. Title.
  BT825.W57 2007
  248.8'6175—dc22
10 9 8 7 6 5   2007000036

Rights for publishing this book outside the U.S.A. or in non-English languages are administered by Gospel Light Worldwide, an international not-for-profit ministry. For additional information, please visit www.glww.org, email info@glww.org, or write to Gospel Light Worldwide, 1957 Eastman Avenue, Ventura, CA 93003, U.S.A.

To Cindi Pursley
for inspiration

For now we see in a mirror dimly,
but then face to face;
now I know in part,
but then I will know fully just as
I also have been fully known.
But now faith, hope, love, abide these three;
but the greatest of these is love.

1 CORINTHIANS 13:12-13, *NASB*

Contents

SECTION THREE:

Using the Pictures

Acknowledgments

My deepest appreciation goes out to the many people who talked with me about their extraordinary experiences. To protect privacy, many names are pseudonyms. However, other persons either gave me permission or asked me to use their names. I appreciate their openness and willingness to be identified. I send my deepest gratitude to Cindi Pursely for sharing so significantly from her nursing career with hospice programs and working with the dying. Her insights remain an inspiration.

Many of theses stories were shared with great emotion and arose from a personal struggle that remains forever. Thank you, friends, for trusting your hearts with me on such a personal level.

Bernice McShane did the arduous task of proofreading. Thanks, Bernie!

As always, I'm grateful to my close friend and agent, Greg Johnson.

Introduction

One of a diminishing handful of survivors of World War I, Jack Oscar recently turned 106 years old. Despite his amazing age, he clearly described his memory of the first man he saw die in the Great War. Jack's memory remained fresh and crisp, and even though he had passed beyond the magic line of 100 years of age, his recollections spilled out of him as if the experience had happened only yesterday.

After shipping out from the white cliffs of Dover, Jack's unit landed on the ocean-swept shores of France. The piercing sounds of machine guns sent him diving for protection from unforgiving bullets flying over his head. Never had he heard such a frightening noise. Bombs exploded in the open fields, causing Jack to cower terrified on the ground, fearing the overpowering roar of the explosions and the flying shrapnel. The acrid smell of gunpowder and smoke ate at his lungs. Nevertheless, his company plowed ahead through the field of dirt and debris.

By mid-day, the British unit came to a hilltop. They had to get over the ridge, and each man knew that death waited on the other side. With icy fear in their hearts, the soldiers made their fearless assault and began tumbling over the crest of the hill. On the other side, Jack stumbled upon the mangled body of a good buddy.

His friend had run down the slope when the German machine guns opened up from the other side of the valley. A blast of heavy fire caught him in the shoulder before the spray of lead tore down his chest and across his body. By the time the soldier dropped to the ground, the remnants of his stomach lay on the ground beside him. The man writhed in pain with more of his abdominal organs outside than in. Jack dropped down beside his friend to see if anything could be done.

"Shoot me!" the wounded soldier screamed. "Please! Take me out of my pain!"

The man's agony was worse than anything Jack could have seen in six lifetimes. He didn't know what to do but started to pull out his pistol to stop this poor man's misery.

Suddenly, the soldier's countenance changed and his whimpering stopped; he reached up and a broad smile broke across his face.

The man softly said one word, "Mother." With a smile on his face, he died peacefully.

Jack shared the last 60 seconds of this man's life, and 88 years later the story remained as vivid as if it had happened only minutes before. Jack also never forgot the fact that this man's mother had died several years before the war. After all of these years, he still believes that the dying man uttered his last word upon seeing his dead mother walk across the French battlefield to take him home.

I will tell you many similar stories.

Through these stories, this book can help you in a number of ways. Each chapter will assist you in dealing with the reality of death. Obviously unavoidable, death remains the ultimate subject we sidestep as long as possible. As long as the deceased is a person down the street, we can keep the topic in the third person. When it becomes a first person issue involving a family member or friend, someone we lived with or know, we shut down. It is the goal of this book to help you change that fear.

Can we get beyond our morbid apprehension concerning the inevitable? Yes. Is a dignified celebration of death possible? I believe so.

Through these stories, my intention is to challenge your perspective and give you a new ease with the inevitable. Will everyone understand these stories that I have observed or agree with my conclusions? No. But they remain as a witness to a reality that exceeds our grasp. In fact, you may be surprised at how positive and hope filled this subject can be.

In many instances, people avoid the hospital or home once they learn that someone is on his or her deathbed, and they may go to great lengths to avoid a conversation or encounter with the dying person. Others develop assumptions that the terminally ill change and no longer need or want the relationships they have enjoyed all their lives. While it is true that death takes us to a different place in our final lap around the track, everyone still needs warmth and caring. My intention is to offer you assurance that your extended hand will still be deeply appreciated by those preparing to leave this world.

Many, many people are unsure of how to talk with a person standing on the threshold of death. The thought of having a conversation with someone who has one foot over the line can feel foreboding or threatening. Consequently, people pretend that the person will not die, or try to ignore the situation altogether. They look the other way and the dying pay the price of loneliness. I believe we can change that picture. By the time you've finished this book, I hope you'll no longer have such feelings. You'll discover that we can easily talk to the dying and discover their final feelings and perceptions.

Our job is to learn how to ask the right questions that will allow the dying to share their inner experiences. You might be surprised to discover what a person will tell you about how it feels to walk through the Valley of the Shadow of Death. I will explore how to appropriately ask those questions.

In order to find the courage to explore these issues, we must be able to think about our own deaths constructively and become comfortable with the idea of our own death. I hope that by the time you finish this book, you will have made peace with the fact of your own demise.

Most of all, I want to offer you a promise that has motivated Christians for centuries. Because of the resurrection of Jesus Christ from the dead, the Church has always proclaimed victory over death. This promise shows us that we do not have to be afraid. Each of us should not only be comfortable with our own demise, but we should also eagerly await this coming transition. Does this sound strange? It shouldn't. The apostles wrote large chunks of the New Testament to explain how this promise can be ours. Their clues can help you find peace with this subject.

My hope is that this book will help you accomplish that purpose once and for all.

Discovering the Picture Album

But as it is, they desire a better country, that is,
a heavenly one. Therefore God is not ashamed to be called their God;
for He has prepared a city for them.

HEBREWS 11:16, *NASB*

During the years I worked as a pastor, it struck me as important to remember these fantastic near-death events I observed, and so, over the years, I began to write the stories down in a notebook reserved for such experiences. As my notes grew, I began to think of them as a collection of photographs, pictures we don't often see when we think about death. Even now I think of each piece of evidence about this phenomenon, whether it's a true story, a passage of Scripture, a piece of research or a hard statistic, like a picture, and each picture forms another piece of what I am calling the picture album. So in this first section, we will take a hard look at the evidence and research offered by near-death experiences for the existence of an afterlife.

Snapshots

On a cold weekend in winter, nurse Cindi Pursely's caseload contained the names of two patients hanging on to the end of their lives but still struggling with an overwhelming fear of dying. Neither of these patients knew each other or ever had any contact.

For more than 28 years Cindi had been a nurse, and for the last 17 she had worked with a hospice organization. Cindi had a passion to help the dying, and in particular, she worried about those patients who fiercely resisted the inevitable. These two patients stood at the top of that list.

A woman in her eighties, Betty Meier had no idea of what lay ahead but she didn't want any part of finding out. Throughout her life, she had dreaded the end, and because of this, Cindi worried about how Betty would complete the final lap of her journey. Betty, who considered herself an agnostic, was one of Cindi's most resistant patients, and this weighed heavily on Cindi's mind.

Al Harris was not quite the same. Only in his late forties when the end of the track came into view, he believed he was far too young to die. Al hated every moment of the inevitable process. He steadfastly refused to talk about what might be "out there" the second after his heart stopped. Al also lived on the agnostic side.

When patients like Al and Betty resist the unavoidable, their final days are often filled with fitful moments of physical and spiritual anxiety. On these hard assignments, Cindi's duties grew more difficult as family members became more and more anxious watching loved ones try to fight off death. Suffice it to say that Cindi wasn't looking forward to her appointments with Betty and Al.

On this particular day, her first visit was to Betty's house. For Cindi, the appointment required a measure of internal resolve.

"You look unusually well this morning," Cindi began her visit. "Genuinely happy."

"I had a wonderful night's sleep," Betty Meier said in a stronger voice than usual. "You'll not believe my amazing experience." Her face remained gray and her hands shook.

"Experience?"

"Yes!" Betty's eyes widened with enthusiasm. "I had almost drifted off to sleep when I slipped off to the other place."

Cindi studied Betty carefully. The stale smell of a sick room hung in the air. The woman sounded like she was hallucinating and Cindi needed to determine her level of orientation. Betty certainly appeared rational enough but maybe she was still out of it. Cindi asked an array of questions: What day was it? Who was the president? Did Betty know what month it was? And Betty sailed through the test. She was clearly in touch with reality.

"I saw the other side," Betty said boldly. Her reddened eyes widened. "Most amazing thing! At first, I thought I was dreaming but then I knew I wasn't. Strangest thing how it happened. Something like going to sleep but no! No! I wasn't dreaming."

Cindi sat down in the chair next to the bed. "Can you tell me what you saw?"

Betty scooted up in the bed. "Two little boys had died. Cutest little guys. Of course, they were little fellows and didn't know where in the world they were. I guess you might say that they had come to this holding realm where people arrive immediately after they die. They just didn't know what in the world to do and were afraid."

Cindi stared at her. Never had Betty Meier given any clues that she even had opinions about whether there was anything on the other side of life. On this morning, her attitude and descriptions had completely changed.

"You can understand how two little boys who had just died would be bewildered," Betty continued. "Their problem was they didn't know how to get across that great divide."

"What did you experience?" Cindi asked cautiously.

"Well, the two little guys seemed so bewildered. Then, they figured out that there was a path out of this holding area they were in. Hand in hand, the two little boys started down that road and it was like heaven broke out in rejoicing. The wind began to blow at their backs. Cindi, it was so wonderful seeing those little boys become happy as they went down that path into eternity. I was so thrilled that all my fears vanished."

"You're not afraid anymore?" Cindi asked.

"Not a bit! I'm ready to go on. Everything is fine."

Cindi Pursely left Betty Meier's house, grappling with what she had just heard. She was delighted Betty had made such progress but didn't know what to make of it. The rest of the day proved arduous with a large number of patients who needed her attention. Cindi's work schedule stretched out into the evening until she came to the last patient, and one she always dreaded to see: Al Harris.

Al's daughter answered the door. She reported hearing a strange sound during the night though the listening device they had installed in Al's bedroom.

"It was a strange sound," she said, "a noise like wind blowing. It sounded like my father was blowing on or at something. Couldn't make anything out of it."

"Hmm." Cindi rubbed her chin thoughtfully. "Is your father asleep now?"

"I don't think so. You can talk to him."

Cindi went back to the bedroom and opened the door slowly. Al was lying in bed with his eyes closed. The door squeaked. He asked her to enter.

"How are you doing this evening?" Cindi asked apprehensively as she stepped into the room.

"Fine," Al said calmly.

"Good." Cindi circled around the bed. Her patient certainly looked better than he had in several days "You seem to be resting better."

"I am."

Cindi reached down to check his pulse. "Heart rate's okay."

"I'm not worried anymore," Al said slowly.

Cindi straightened up. "I don't understand."

"Last night I had one of those twilight experiences I've heard about. Never had one before."

"Last night?"

Al nodded his head. "I saw two little boys. Little ones that had lost their way."

Cindi stiffened. "Where?" she asked cautiously.

"Trying to get into eternity. In that realm where I guess you go right after you die. They weren't sure how to get out of there. Then, they found this path and I started blowing as hard as I could to help them go forward. The wind picked up. As I watched them find their way down that route into eternity, my own fears disappeared."

Al kept talking, telling the exact story that Cindi had heard when she started her day hours ago. Betty Meier and Al Harris, who lived miles apart and had never met or talked to each other, had experienced exactly the same event in eternity. In addition to that, Betty and Al no longer feared death, and both ceased to be agnostic.

Astonishing? Not to many of the people who regularly work with the dying.

Snapshots of the Other Side

While not everyone has an experience than can be heard with the ears or observed with the eyes, many dying people experience events similar to Betty and Al. If we listen and observe carefully, the dying can teach us important things that we need to learn in preparing for the end of our own life's journey.

During my years in seminary, I studied the Bible in the original languages and wrestled with the meaning of the text. My professors wanted me to formulate my own opinions about what the Bible taught, but I noticed that no one talked about death. In time, I came to feel that it was almost a taboo subject. Some debated the resurrection of Jesus of Nazareth while others argued about the Old Testament experiences. However, no professor or student had anything to say or teach personally about his or her own experiences with death. Their cameras weren't open. Death was a closed subject.

In my own scrutiny of the Scriptures, I recognized that the Bible didn't present a systematic teaching about the afterlife. Rather, the scriptural offerings were again more like a photo album of snapshots taken across centuries of history. The stories in Scripture appeared without much elaboration: just simple photos taken at cemeteries or bedsides. The work of making sense out of the snapshots and trying to fit the pictures together in some appropriate order was left to us.

In the Old Testament, we find many strange stories, such as Samuel reappearing from the dead when Saul visited the witch of Endor. Shadrack, Meshack and Abednego worked through a fiery death. Elijah restored a widow's dead son to life. We have a few stories of people returning from the dead but nothing like what we find in the New Testament when Jesus brought life to many of the dying. Certainly, the story of dead Lazarus being raised after three days in the tomb stupefied the first observers. The ultimate resurrection of Jesus Christ from the dead became the normative event for all Christian theology.

Developing the most extensive systematization in the Bible, the apostle Paul took these events and made projections in his writing to the Corinthian church. His entire system of beliefs grew out of his conviction that Jesus Christ won the great victory over death. The problem of his first-century readers was in understanding how to allow the same convictions to empower their own perspectives. How could they make sense of these events?

As the centuries went by, the Church arranged the pictures in the photo album according to the dictates of theologians. When the Protestant Reformation exploded, different theological voices started jockeying for higher ground and, as a result, the photo album landed upside down. A wide range of ideas sprang up, ranging from the Roman Catholic Church's teaching on purgatory to the Southern Baptist conviction that the stories of Lazarus, the rich man, and Abraham give us the assurance of an immediate entrance into eternity after death. Sometimes, the theologian's pictures became so confusing that it was hard to make any sense out of the resulting theology.

Today, we are the recipients of a disordered picture album.

This book is not another attempt to put the album back in a final order. Rather, it is written to help you find the same joy and assurance that the Bettys and Als of the world have discovered. And I want you to know that the photographs *are still being taken today*. I think you'll be surprised by how often these unusual experiences happen. My hunch is that you'll find comfort.

Written from the position of orthodox Christian faith, this book will not attempt to intrude into a realm where God has not invited us. Rather, I am only following where the experiences of others have led. Ultimately, everyone must travel through the nebulous gates of time, and for many, it has already proved to be a good journey. How can I be so sure? I have the snapshots to prove it.

Learning to Handle the Unexpected

For a number of years, I taught a course covering the entire Bible at the University of Victoria in Canada. Usually, the people who attended these sessions were ministers from every denomination who had come to be trained in biblical literacy. Near the end of the New Testament section, I talked about the Gospel stories and their recording of Jesus' resurrection. Because I believe the intention of these stories to be personal, I tried to relate the material in a manner that had poignancy. Usually nerves were touched.

After one of these sessions, a tall, handsome, blonde-haired pastor named George came forward with tears in his eyes. He pulled me aside and told me the story of the crib death of his infant son. George and his wife had gone to a church meeting and left the baby in the nursery. As his session concluded, George heard a scream and knew it was his wife's voice. He rushed back to the nursery and found her holding their son, who was now dead.

The death nearly killed him. Night after night, they would go to bed without being able to sleep. After six months, the situation had not improved. On one of these difficult nights, he stretched out in bed without much hope of a decent night's sleep. As George drifted off into that same twilight zone Al Harris experienced, he suddenly saw a large, strong man standing at the foot of his bed. The blond-haired adult dressed in a white robe looked at him with intense scrutiny.

George lay stunned, staring at this figure he'd never seen before.

"You don't know me?" the man said.

George shook his head.

"I am your son. You brought me into this world but I only needed to stay a short time. I have been spared from the adversities this world dispenses and have now entered eternity free

22

from error. You have nothing to fear, nothing over which to have anguish. Sleep well and fret not for we shall meet again."

In that moment, the son was gone and George knew he had not been dreaming. In a way that he never would have expected, George had been given a photograph of his baby who had become a man in eternity. Could he make sense out of what had transpired? Did he understand everything that was ahead? Was he able to have unique insight into tomorrow? No. But George slept peacefully and knew the future beyond his death would be positive. He never again had a problem sleeping.

Paying Attention to the Pictures

How can we make sense out of these experiences that surface at the end of life? One question people ask is, How many people have experienced some sort of near encounter with death? Surveys taken in the United States indicate that approximately 15 million people have had such an experience.[1]

Once unreported, reports of near-death experiences now seem to be everywhere. One-third of resuscitated people return with reports of the other side after having lost all of their vital signs. From the medical profession, Melvin Morse, M.D., reported that 70 percent of children facing the end of their lives also experienced a near-death experience.[2] The frequency of these experiences tells us that a significant number of people have been beyond the border of life.

When the International Association for Near-Death Studies investigated people who felt they had experienced eternity in some form, they explored how close these individuals had come to an actual death. Of the 229 people who responded to the questionnaire, 23 percent had been diagnosed as clinically dead, while 40 percent were diagnosed as critically ill. Another 37 percent reported an extraordinary experience in an environment that wasn't life threatening.[3] While these experiences differ, they suggest that the edge of life may be fuzzier than we thought. At least, we can observe that unexpected experiences seem to punch holes in time that let us gaze through to the other side.

One of the observations gained from these experiences appears to be that friends almost universally observe a dramatic change in the person's perspective after they come back. As we observed earlier with Al Harris and Betty Meier, their view of life and death was changed forever. The same is true of people who survive near-death experiences. Often they will develop an entirely new set of ethics or values, or change employment. They become more concerned for others, and friends report that they are more sensitive than before. Looking over the edge *does* change people.

That ought to cause us to take a hard look at this subject.

The problem is that we write off the dying like we might an old car that no longer runs well. We think all usefulness is gone. We love them and want their last hours to be as peaceful as possible but nothing is expected. Their task is to die; our job is to turn out the lights after they're gone.

No one expects that with their last breath a dying person might teach the world lessons of profound meaning. Recently a dear friend of over 30 years called me to say that she was dying and wanted me to officiate at her funeral. The request was factual, to the point, and had the same emotional tone as if she were asking me to drop by the store and pick up a loaf of bread. We talked over the phone and I immediately went to her house. Nathalee and I talked like old friends at a class reunion. In a matter of a couple of weeks, Nat was gone, but during that time I relearned some important insights.

Initially, Nathalee reminded me once again that the dying are trying to teach us if only we pay attention. Nathalee wanted me to understand what she was experiencing, and though her body was wearing out, her intentions remained strong. I have observed this with many people. If we learn to listen intently and observe what is happening, they'll contribute important data for our own journey.

In recent years a new movement to help people die at home has emerged in America. Hospice organizations offer personal care and medical services that provide the terminally ill with an alternative to a hospital. Not only are families saved considerable expense, but also the dying can spend their last few weeks or months in an environment that is familiar and personal. During their visits, hospice workers have learned to observe what the dying may teach.

While working with hospice social workers, nurses and chaplains, I discovered that hospice organizations also contribute a significant base of important data. Skilled workers accumulate their own set of experiences that are consistent with the discoveries of the Betty Meiers, Al Harrises, Nathalees and Georges of the world. Dipping into this reservoir of knowledge added important dimensions to my observations, and the consistent theme here is simply that we need to listen closely.

Paying Attention

The art of listening isn't easy with the living, much less with the dying. We are far too engrossed in our own struggles to catch what goes flying past our ears. Often, we're not good at asking the right questions to help the dying express themselves. Many times we retreat and duck out the back door or run from the deathbed scene. The result is that the dying struggle through the process alone.

As we will discuss more fully in a later chapter, few of us know how to offer physical assistance to help ease this time of transition. With our eyes wide open, we assume that discourse with the dying is like exchanging straightforward factual data. But once we lie down and close our eyes, we drift off into another world of many shapes and sizes called dreamland. Without expecting the expressions that arise from this world of shadows to mean much, we dismiss our dreams as being little more than aberrations. The truth is that dreams are often worlds of symbolic communication filled with important meaning. It takes time and energy to figure out what is going on. The dying often experience dreamlike symbolism and may speak from this form of understanding.

So in this context, listening means learning to hear someone's inner world and deepest feelings with far greater attention in order that we don't let our own assumptions get in the way. The dying may speak in images far more akin to dreamland than the world of everyday reality. In order to understand them, we have to make adjustments to comprehend a poetic form of expression that is sometimes elusive but actually far more expressive than the world of facts.

In later chapters, we will look more deeply at how we can accomplish this task.

Stop the Resistance

When someone from across the street dies, or someone we don't know, we're able to exercise considerable objectivity. However, having a person we deeply love die in our own house or in our own family is another matter. When the death is close at hand, observers often go into a mode of denial, trying to resist the fact that the death also involves them. Sometimes resistance turns into a stone wall when the companion or friend realizes that the tolling bell will someday ring for him or her.

Several years ago, nurse Cindi Pursely received an assignment with a warning attached. Marion Black had been diagnosed as terminal and needed help, but the real problem was her husband. George Black didn't want in any form to acknowledge that his wife was ill. Every mirror had been removed from their house and the man forbade even the mention of the word "cancer" by anyone. How was the nurse to be of assistance in a house sitting under a gigantic "No"?

When Cindi arrived, George Black met her at the front door and warned her that no one was to suggest that a problem existed in their house. The social worker had already warned Cindi that the man was erratic and could easily become a major source of trouble.

Cindy walked into Marion's bedroom and quickly surveyed the situation. Did George Black really think that his wife couldn't tell how jaundiced her skin had become? Did he consider that she wouldn't know her abdomen was significantly distended? Every aspect of her terminal condition seemed obvious.

Sitting down next to the bed, Cindi asked a simple question: "How are you?"

"I am dying," Marion Black answered frankly.

George Black went ballistic! He blamed Cindi for breaking confidence and disclosing the "big secret." Did he really think his wife didn't know? Afraid so! In the following weeks, George Black even tried to get Cindi's nursing license revoked. Of course he failed, but George Black remains a prime example of destructive denial.

Beyond Denial

We don't have to retreat or panic. We can stand at the edge of life without fear. The experiences of the dying offer us evidence that we will not walk through death alone. If friends and relatives are not with us when we die, through these stories we see that others are standing by on the other side waiting to help.

I'm like anyone else. I've been reluctant to think about my own death. I read the Scripture and hear the reassuring promises. However, there is a fine line between an idea and our personal grasp of that very same truth. Our perception has to be accurate if we are going to "get inside" a truth and make it our own. It's one thing to hear a reassuring sermon about death or dying and quite another to lie down for the last time in our own bed.

As I've reviewed these "snapshots" of the other side, they have radically changed my perception. In fact, the stories of these encounters have given me new assurance that supports the biblical promises I've long believed in.

Hope for Hopeless Times

When my wife's father died, everyone who knew Mitchell Brantley felt the loss. A man of principle and honor, Mitch had always been an excellent Christian gentleman. My wife,

Margueritte, particularly felt the pain of her father's death, as did her siblings. Due to her own deep sense of grief, their elderly Aunt Joan couldn't attend the funeral. Mitch had taken care of his wife's sister through the years after his own wife's death and his passing proved to be more than Joan could bear.

Joan moved into St. Ann's nursing home not long after and much of the time she needed a walker just to get around. Her afternoon walks down the long halls helped her stay flexible, although she continued to struggle with depression and loneliness. On one of these afternoons, Joan had been wrestling intensely with dejection and loneliness. She hobbled down the hallway with her hands firmly on the walker while her mind was lost in deep reflection. The deaths of her sister and brother-in-law had stripped her of the closeness she had always felt with family during her life. Joan's only surviving sister lived out of the state and they could only talk periodically on the phone for short times.

As she trudged down the hall, Joan abruptly realized that someone was walking beside her. Expecting it to be one of the other patients, she looked beside her. In that moment, Joan knew who was there. She looked again and saw Mitch standing beside her. There was no question in her mind that it was him, and she immediately knew that he was checking on her as he had done for years during his life. To her surprise, he seemed to be dressed as he usually had been, wearing one of his favorite caps that he always wore when he walked. For several moments, Joan was certain of his presence. Then, he was gone.

The heaviness she felt previously disappeared, and Joan continued her walks with a strong sense of personal reassurance that she was being looked after by her brother-in-law. Was this unusual experience real? For Joan, it was filled with as much reality as any experience in her life. Did it help? Absolutely.

Are such events common? At least 15 million Americans say yes. Our task is to be aware of these experiences and then try to understand their affirmation.

Notes

1. International Association for Near-Death Studies, P.O. Box 502, East Windsor Hall, CT 06028-0502, email: office@jands.org.
2. Ibid.
3. Ibid.

CHAPTER THREE

Final Tasks

Jake Alexander had always been a tough guy, able to withstand pain and injury. During his years as a soldier in Vietnam, Jake lived through many battles and conflicts in remote towns and in dense, forbidding jungles. Several times his unit found themselves pinned down by enemy fire. During these nightmares of battle, death stared him in the naked eye, and Jake saw the atrocities that left their marks on many good American young men. Jake was tough, but he was also marked by his experience.

During one of those forays through the dense undergrowth and thick clusters of towering trees, the Viet Cong struck with unexpected ferocity, holding the Americans down and preparing to wipe out Jake's entire outfit. Believing they were in a hopeless situation, the commanding officer called in an air attack on their position as a last ditch effort to stop the enemy. Jets came diving through the clouds, spraying the jungle with everything from bullets and rockets to balls of fire. By the time the attack was over, the enemy had been incinerated as well as most of the American troops. The trees were decimated and turned black from the explosive blasts. Agent Orange had scorched acres of the jungle and had cleared out the enemy as well.

To the surprise of everyone including himself, Jake Alexander crawled away from the battle scene. One of the few survivors, he sustained severe wounds from the battle and the bombardment. Eventually, Jake returned to the United States with hopes of resuming his life like any normal citizen. Unfortunately, what Jake had seen in Vietnam wouldn't stay on the other side of the ocean. His war days had been too volatile to simply go away like a cloud of smoke. Although he was never diagnosed, Jake likely suffered from Post-Traumatic Stress disorder. The old memories kept returning with a vividness that terrified him as he relived these deadly encounters on a daily basis.

The only thing that Jake could understand to do with the pain was drink more heavily. His endless hours drinking in bars and alone in his bedroom led to alcoholism and only added to his emotional damage. As bad as his war memories were, it took a couple of decades before the worst effects of Vietnam set in. No one had told Jake, or any of the other soldiers, that Agent Orange often left harsh residual effects. It took a while before the full results set in for Jake, but contact with Agent Orange eventually led to cancer.

When he ended up in a Veterans Administration hospital, the doctors immediately discovered the cancer. Jake had cancer of the tonsils and the condition would prove fatal. Surgeons had to cut out half of Jake's tongue to slow the growth of the malignant area in his throat. He could still talk but his voice came out somewhat distorted, sounding garbled. Because of the disastrous events and consequences of his life, Jake no longer trusted anyone. The family realized that they needed someone who had the ability to help him regain some of his confidence before he died. That's when they contacted a hospice organization.

The hospice assigned Cindi Pursely the task of trying to re-establish a significant relationship with this disillusioned man. While it took longer than usual, eventually Cindi broke through the protective shell Jake had constructed around his life. She encouraged him and got him to talk with her, but by this point Jake was well into his last lap around the track. Much of the time Cindi was with him, he disappeared, lost in mental aberrations leading him to believe he was back in Vietnam fighting the enemy.

When he came out of these fog banks, Jake would clutch Cindi's hand tightly. "I've got to get to Kissinger!" he'd yell in surprisingly clear diction. "Got to get an important message to Kissinger!" He'd stare blankly into Cindi's eyes and would then drop back onto the bed unconscious.

Going back and forth out of his Vietnam experiences induced long moments of disorientation. But Jake was certain he had an extremely important task to complete before he died, as if he had information that he must get to the U.S. Secretary of State. He wasn't in bed dying. Jake was still in Vietnam with a job to complete.

Tasks to Be Completed

The world has changed. Medieval society tended to focus on the end of life, so much so that medieval-age monks would sleep in caskets to familiarize themselves with the feel of their final resting place. Death remained too omnipresent not to pay careful attention. In an age without significant anesthesia or antiseptics, pain remained the curse of human existence.

Everyone had to watch for whatever was coming because death could leap out unexpectedly from any street corner at any given moment.

The contemporary world looks in the opposite direction. With plastic surgeons on every street corner waiting with syringes filled with Botox, we try to perpetuate the look of being 20 years old for eternity. Old age is out and no one wants to visit a funeral home. "Death" is now the word you're not supposed to say. Don't think about the departing. We can't imagine that the dying could have any significant work left to do.

The truth of the matter is that they have a great deal to finish up, whether they have work to do internally or externally by resolving issues with family or friends.

Take Jake Alexander for instance. Jake's war experience had severely disrupted his entire life. Not much had turned out right. Agent Orange had begun a process in his body and he died because of it. But Jake didn't think he was through until he got his final message to the "big boss" in Washington. Jake may have had some internal issues left to resolve.

If we are going to understand what the dying can teach us, we can't negate what they are saying by suggesting their talk is little more than crazy hallucinations, though it's true that sometimes the terminally ill will spin stories that are purely from their imaginations. Without question, medicines and debilitating illnesses can induce strange reactions. The problem is that often times the living tend to write off *everything* that comes out of the mouths of the dying as nothing more than an overheated imagination. Their strength is fading. Never mind the babbling. Stay focused on what is in front of your eyes. Unfortunately, this can also be a negation of potential insights being offered by those standing on the threshold of death.

As the dying make their initial preparations to cross over, there often seems to be work yet for them to complete. Instead of retreating, we must discover how to lean forward, hear their ideas and respond with insight. As they finish their tasks and work through whatever they must before the end of their lives, they have the capacity to teach us much about our own lives.

Individual Differences

The process of dying differs with each person as much as our fingerprints are unique. No two people have the same agenda in stepping over the ultimate line. However, observing the process can be uniquely instructive. While our life's experiences are different from anyone else's, we need to develop a sense of what's going on if we are to sort out our own material with greater ease.

What occurs during the process of dying is conditioned by how we lived. Human beings universally experience things that can be extremely difficult to reflect upon. Perhaps the dying person will be haunted by a past moral indiscretion. Then again, the person may have been the victim of the cruelty of other people. Possibly the untimely death of a parent or sibling has left us in a suspended state of grief. We may not talk about it but the memory might still be there . . . floating.

Floating. There's a word to ponder.

While we might not describe our own past in this way, the truth is that past events can linger in our minds like clouds that never completely drifted by. Over the years perhaps we kept pushing the clouds away, thinking another night or two and they'd be gone when we woke up. A couple of nights turned into decades while these hovering stormy reminders still await resolution. The dying may sometimes try to resolve this mist and smog before they go.

The sounds, the words and the broken sentences that are often considered nothing more than an emotional aberration at the time of death may actually be an attempt to resolve what has remained from these floating remnants of the past. The truth is that we will die much as we have lived, except that we will no longer be able to hide from what we've concealed. Yesterday will return to center stage and take priority, regardless of the major news story that is consuming the world's current interest.

The conclusion of these unresolved problems has a direct bearing on how people die. The Jake Alexanders of the world may have had more struggles during their lifetimes than anyone deserves, but in the final hours they are still on a mission to get matters settled. If we pay attention to this process, we can stop and consider our own issues more carefully while our bones and muscles remain strong. Getting things resolved today certainly makes it easier to finish up matters at the end of life.

Going to the Movies

When Victor Parks began to die, he would lie for hours with his eyes closed. Most of the family assumed he was slipping in and out of a final coma. Finally, the visiting nurse realized she should get some sense of what was going on. When Vic's eyelids fluttered, she pushed the issue.

"You're awake?" the nurse asked.

"Sure," Vic said. "Never really been asleep."

"Really?" the nurse answered. "The family thought you'd been unconscious."

"They're wrong. I just tuned them out."

"Well, what are you doing lying there with your eyes closed?"

Vic opened his eyes wide. "I'm watching the movies. They are absolutely fascinating. All-consuming."

"The movies?" The nurse's voice rose an octave. "What movies?"

"The ones in my head. I'm watching the scenes of my life being replayed. The show is going on right now and I'm experiencing it. The cinema is right behind my eyes. Of course, some of the scenes are a little ragged and I have to slow them down. Have to stop and work out the issues. Then, we go on again."

"The pictures are in your head?"

"Absolutely, and they are running right now. All I have to do is close my eyes and I can watch them once again. They never stop."

"Amazing," the nurse said.

"Sure." Vic closed his eyes again. "See! They're going full tilt. Tell my family that this is my private showing and I'm doing quite fine without them. Don't worry. I'll let you know when I have something to say."

Victor Parks continued in that state for several days. Even though he gave the appearance of being comatose, he certainly wasn't. Vic was simply too busy studying his films and running the instant replays to interrupt his show with casual conversations. His time was running out and he didn't want interruptions from the family. When he finally died, the smile on his face seemed to say he'd finally reviewed all the reels and was happy with the edited final cut. The work was done. Vic could leave.

We must not assume that the quietness of the dying means that the telephone line is dead and no communication is going through. The truth may be far from it.

The Final Scene

Ben Harris had a case history much like Jake Alexander. Both were Vietnam vets and had crawled into some of the worst situations the world offers. Consequently, Ben experienced "pop-ups," his way of describing flashback experiences that left him feeling totally paranoid.

Living like a hermit, Ben would sit out in the garage in an old lawn chair when he knew the flashbacks were coming. The pop-ups happened throughout the day and were always filled with violence. They didn't stop when Ben got the diagnosis that he didn't have long to live in this world. In fact, the experiences of the past seemed to become more frequent, which only added to his paranoia and made it difficult for him to distinguish between reality and fantasy. But Ben Harris knew he had work to do. Pushing everything else aside, he set out to make peace with these past events erupting in his imagination. As his death approached, Ben faced the mental and emotional battles with these events that had happened three decades earlier. He struggled with the contents and wrestled with the implications of what had happened to him so many years prior. In the end, Ben Harris died peacefully. He became kind and gentle in a way he had not been before. His work was done and Ben could go on.

Ben, Vic and Jake are examples for us to remember. They are people who had struggles but through their conflicts taught the people around them how important it was to get the work done.

The Mysteries of Life (and Death)

Death wasn't particularly on my mind when I began a conversation with a friend who had taken on the task of bringing spiritual discipline to my life. During my quest for answers, Gene Warr had been referred to me as a layman dedicated to the truth. As a young man I had been confronted with the Christian story and had come to the conclusion that my acceptance hinged on the validity of the resurrection account of the raising of Jesus Christ from the dead. If Jesus had conquered death, I would be a fool not to accept this event. On the other hand, if the story wasn't true, then the entire Christian message was a deception and I should look somewhere else.

After arduous exploration and analysis, I concluded that Jesus had knocked the door down between this world and the next. But then what? How was I to view death? A parachurch organization I was in touch with suggested that Gene Warr could help me with the answers.

In those days, Gene's office could be found in downtown Oklahoma City. I walked in and the secretary ushered me into the inner office. After my questions, Gene whipped out a Bible (as he always did) and started explaining. He said the best place to begin was 1 John 5:11-13, which states:

And this is the testimony: that God has given us eternal life, and this life is in His Son. He who has the Son has life; he who does not have the Son of God does not have life. These things I have written to you who believe in the name of the Son of God, that you may continue to believe in the name of the Son of God.

Gene thumped on the page. "God said it. I believe it. That settles it." That was Gene's way. The matter was concluded.

It wasn't quite that easy for me, especially with a background in secular philosophy, three years studying the Greek language, and a good case of agnosticism, but I understood Gene's point. The Bible is quite clear that eternal life is a gift that comes with knowing Jesus Christ. If we know Him, then this gift is a part of the encounter.

When I studied the entire Bible, I found an unfolding story of how the biblical ancients' understanding of death had developed. Originally, death was not a part of the divine plan but came on the scene through the sinfulness of humanity. The first believers called Jesus the "Second Adam" because He reversed the deadly error of Adam and Eve and brought new life to the world. The culmination of the Bible came through Jesus' teaching: "I am the resurrection and the life. Those who believe in Me, though he may die, he shall live. And whoever lives and believes in Me shall never die" (John 11:25-26). The appearance, teaching, death and resurrection of Jesus of Nazareth was the climax of all the prophecies of the Old Testament.

Certainly the Old Testament warned against contact with necromancy or anyone attempting to make contact with the dead. Saul received a harsh judgment for attempting to contact the dead Samuel through the intervention of the witches at Endor. Severe condemnation, including death, was pronounced on such practices. However, I was surprised to discover that many Christians would have nothing to do with near-death experiences because they interpreted them in light of passages like Leviticus 20:27:

> A man or a woman who is a medium, or who has famil-iar spirits, shall surely be put to death; they shall stone them with stones. Their blood shall be upon them.

Or Deuteronomy 18:10-11:

> There shall not be found among you anyone who makes his son or his daughter pass through the fire, or one who practices witchcraft, or a soothsayer, or one who inter-prets omens, or a sorcerer, or one who conjures spells, or a medium, or a spiritist, or one who calls up the dead.

Even ministers who have had near-death experiences and have talked about them publicly could wind up in trouble with their congregation or denomination. These ministers did not contact wizards or spirit-guides or use witchcraft to make con-tact with the long dead. These events simply happened to peo-ple who nearly died and experienced something extraordinary. Like emotions or opinions, an experience can't be right or wrong. We have to look into what occurred to understand the meaning of the event.

As we read the stories of people who momentarily looked and lived beyond the end of life, I want to make sure that you are aware of the convictions that stand behind this book. Proper orientation is appropriate. Unless we stay balanced and clear, we can spin off into strange interpretations that may not make sense. Our task in this book is to remain in harmony with Scripture from beginning to end. I absolutely believe that Jesus Christ brought us the gift of eternal life and I want to understand as fully as I can what this means.

After much exploration and detailed study, I developed the conviction that these stories brought back from afterlife experiences can actually confirm the Scriptures and enlarge our understanding of the Bible. Let's look further at the heart of the matter.

What Is Life?

I don't know.

And I don't know anyone who knows what the *physical essence* of life actually is.

I can give you scientific data that can determine if a person is alive or explain why he or she died. We all understand what happens when the heart stops or breathing quits. Sure, we know what a dead animal looks like as well as a deceased human being. But what is that "thing" that creates the difference between one state and the other? What makes a person alive? And what leaves the body when life stops? We can only say that person died and give a medical diagnosis of what stopped his or her vital functions. But we don't know if his or her organs gave out or if a person's soul left his or her body.

Life is an exceedingly mysterious force that defies description and understanding. Like trying to catch a handful of wind, no one has been able to obtain a bottle full of "life." We find such tales as the Frankenstein story to be so fascinating because they suggest that lightning, or a chemical potion, or unique surgery, can make an inanimate creature return to life. Of course, that's impossible and that is what makes the story fascinating. In the end, we are left at the same point where our ancestors were centuries ago. No one knows what life *actually* is.

The Bible suggests this fact in a number of ways. Scripture describes Jesus Christ as the embodiment of the life force that is also *eternal* life. The power that creates all human existence came through Him. Those who embraced Him by faith received "Life." Yet what is eternal life? A force? An existence? Does it transform me from being physical into a spiritual being? Does my present haircut and beard come with the package? Sorry, the Bible doesn't tell us. We don't fully understand this essence and probably never will this side of eternity, but the promise remains true.

The point? In this scientific age where we have microscopes that can magnify up to a million times, and paleontologists who can probe the earth for insights from millions of years behind us, we still live in an age of mystery where the fundamental answers about existence elude us. We like to think of ourselves as a people of facts, figures and functions but our grasp of what motivates galaxies to move through space still escapes us. Life is a mystery, and this mystery is a fact of human existence. We need to stay in touch with this important insight to stay oriented.

If these things are true of life, *then how much more are they true of death?*

Because we have no means of probing what happens to "who we are" after we die, we are even more amazed when the mystery beyond death opens up unexpectedly for some people. All we can do is try to discern the meaning of what they have experienced. We must try to understand the fact that we can't explain the end of life with a test tube and a slide rule. Mystery hovers around us and is as much a part of life as death. In fact, history has often turned on events that sound like they came from a novelist's pen.

Consider Winston Churchill's situation.

During World War II, Churchill became the living symbol of the British defiance of Nazi intentions. During the bombings of London, this courageous Christian man walked resolutely through the streets without hesitancy. However, Churchill shared with his inner circle that he had a mysterious inner voice that seemed to keep him alert to imminent danger. When the voice warned of impending danger, Churchill listened to it.

For example, while entertaining three government ministers at 10 Downing Street, Winston Churchill suddenly got up from the table and disappeared into the kitchen. An air raid howled outside but up to that moment Churchill had paid it no attention; but now something had changed. On one side of the kitchen a large glass window opened to a view of the garden outside. Churchill immediately told the butler and the maid to leave the kitchen and to go to a bomb shelter. Once they were gone, he went back to his guests and continued talking. Three minutes later a bomb fell behind the house and completely destroyed the kitchen, while Churchill and his guests remained unharmed. Churchill heard the voice speak.

On another occasion, Churchill had been inspecting several gunners when he returned to his car. As always, the door stood open, waiting for him to take his usual seat. This time, however, he stopped and thought for a moment and then, uncharacteristically, went around to the other side of the car. As the vehicle returned through blacked-out streets, a bomb exploded, lifting the car and causing it to careen upward on two wheels. Because Churchill was on the other side of the car, there was no damage to him. When his wife asked about why this had all taken place, Churchill explained that his inner voice had told him to make such a change and he had done so immediately. His life had been spared.[1]

Mystery? Certainly. An inner voice (whether it be intuition or the Holy Spirit) isn't explainable to the world of logical positivism or scientism. But these mysterious experiences happen every day. Appreciating them is an important part of our getting oriented to the unknown in this world, and in the world after this one. We have to keep an open mind, especially when talking about life and death. It was Albert Einstein who said, "The most beautiful thing we can experience is the mysterious. It is the source of all true art and science."[2]

A Surprise Visit

The following story is another example of the great mysteries we find in both life and death. I will tell you many such stories over the course of this book, and many of them, like this one, sound as if they come directly from the New Testament. My conviction is that God the Father has given us additional evidence in these snapshots from beyond. I believe they are part of seeing through a mirror dimly and are intended for our consolation.

Few Christians in recent centuries have had such a reputation for honesty, insightfulness and intelligence as has C. S. Lewis. Well into his academic career at Oxford University, Lewis was a critical thinker and an agnostic as well as a scholar of medieval literature. *Surprised by Joy* is the story of his conversion, and millions have read the book. Both his fiction and non-fiction books remain bestsellers today. During his long career, even people who didn't agree with Lewis or his theology trusted him.

For a period of time, Lewis's death got lost in the back of newspapers because Lewis died the same day that President John F. Kennedy was assassinated. The swirl of stories about the violent death of an American president absorbed the headlines for months and years. C. S. Lewis quietly disappeared. However, the story of his death eventually surfaced, creating an amazing reaction around the world.

The Rev. J. B. Phillips has become a household name for his translation of the New Testament into modern English. Well before the rash of new translations appeared, Phillips had recognized the value of changing the old *King James Version* from formal, dated English into a contemporary expression. The *Phillips* translation had been an international achievement and was part of what started the '70s and '80s rush to retranslate the Scriptures with accuracy and fidelity according to the most ancient manuscripts.

Unfortunately, Phillips had problems with his health. The effect of his lingering illness had created doubt as to whether he should go forward with work on the Old Testament. Rev. Phillips wrestled back and forth with the options. After all, England was still emerging from the devastations of World War II and stores still had bare shelves. Maybe he had exceeded the limits of his own strength. Possibly he ought not to keep up the rigorous task of attempting to translate the Old Testament with its difficult Hebrew context.

Sitting at his desk thinking about the problem, Phillips got up and walked over to the fire that his housekeeper had built in the fireplace in his office and slumped down in a heavy, well-padded chair in front of the warm fire. A similar chair stood only a few feet away. He stared into the flames and thought about the strain of continued translation of the Bible. His thoughts totally absorbed him and he lost track of everything else in the room.

Abruptly a voice interrupted Phillips's contemplation. He looked up and, to his shock, saw that his old friend C. S. Lewis was sitting in the other chair smiling at him.

"I want to encourage you," Dr. Lewis began. "You have important work to do."

J. B. Phillips stared. He hadn't even heard Lewis come into the room. Good heavens! His personal problems had so gripped his mind that he lost touch with what was happening in his own office. Had he been thinking aloud? He didn't think so.

Lewis continued a careful description of how important the *Phillips* translation had proved to be. He didn't think that Phillips fully appreciated the impact his work had made on multitudes. Dr. Lewis suggested he reconsider ceasing the work.

Phillips was startled by such urging and admitted that maybe he should rethink the matter. He told Lewis that he would do so immediately.

"Good," C. S. Lewis said. "I believe this is the right course for you to take."

J. B. Phillips looked back into the fire. Because he had always deeply admired Lewis, he took his words with great seriousness. After several moments of reflection, he turned back to Lewis only to discover that his chair was empty. The man was gone!

Phillips leaped up and ran for the housekeeper, thinking it strange that he had seen Lewis neither come nor go. When had the woman let Lewis in?

"When did C. S. Lewis arrive and leave?" Phillips asked the astonished woman.

"I have no idea what you are talking about," the housekeeper said. "I didn't see Mr. Lewis."

"You didn't let him in?" Phillips's mouth dropped.

The woman shook her head. "No idea what you're talking about." She shrugged. "Didn't see Mr. Lewis leave either."

"Get on the phone immediately," Phillips instructed. "I want you to call Dr. Lewis's residence and find out what is going on."

The woman nodded and left to make the telephone call. Phillips returned to his desk. What in the world was going on? Lewis had been there as clearly as the sun came up that morning. How could the housekeeper not have seen him enter or leave?

Suddenly the door opened again and the housekeeper came in. Her face looked troubled, uncertain, with a twist of astonishment Phillips had never seen before with the woman.

"I talked to his housekeeper," the woman said. "She told me that Mr. Lewis died an hour ago."

Staying Grounded

I first heard this account years ago while I was working in London. When the story appeared in *Guidepost* magazine, millions of Americans read it, and anyone acquainted with the works of Phillips and Lewis couldn't write it off as nonsense. As we orient ourselves to study this subject even deeper, I believe we can see how stories like this one can inspire hope and faith in our own lives, and in the lives of millions of others.

Will these stories produce faith? Actually, I don't believe that's the point. Faith is something you have to come to on your own and is a matter of personal decision. However, I believe these snapshots are meant to help the faithful maintain the course they are on. When Gene Warr read to me in his office these words from John's first letter, "that you may know that you have eternal life," the purpose was to give me an assurance that my personal destiny was sealed whether or not I fully realized it. I didn't have to live my life worrying what waited at the end.

And that's an orientation worth paying attention to.

Notes

1. "Winston Churchill's Inner Voice," *Mysteries of the Unexplained* (Pleasantville, NY: The Reader's Digest Association, 1982), pp. 28-29.
2. Ibid., p. 7.

Patterns and Stages

As we established earlier, at least 15 million people have reported experiencing something extraordinary at the edge of life. So what's really out there? Is there any pattern or predictable systematization to these encounters? Do these experiences follow any particular or consistent order?

In chapter 2, we noted that a near-death study reported that 37 percent of responders had this afterlife journey under circumstances that were not in any way life-threatening. These people also indicated that their encounters felt just as real and were just as life changing as those who had their extraordinary events in a near-death situation. The report suggests that people can have these glimpses into eternity without being ready to die. In other words, you don't have to be on board an airliner plunging toward the earth, or deteriorating in a hospital emergency room, in order to cross the line. However, nothing seems to tell us why some people have the experience and others don't. But formal study in this field is a relatively new endeavor and, therefore, evidence is limited and hard to process scientifically. And most of us still have a lot to learn about the patterns, stages and phenomenon observed in the dying or in near-death survivors.

Chapter Five

How Awareness Begins

We started thinking about these matters seriously when medical doctor Elisabeth Kubler-Ross wrote her ground-breaking book *On Death and Dying* in 1969, which described how the dying prepare themselves for death. She discovered five universal steps that the dying often work through on their way to a peaceful passing. After a diagnosis of death, the patient denies the possibility, which is step one. This is followed by anger, step two. Then, in step three, the person begins attempting to bargain for more time to complete this, that, or the other thing. When the person realizes there is no bargaining chip in this final game, he or she becomes depressed, step four. Once that person has worked through his or her depression, he or she reaches step five, which is acceptance, and the person dies in peace.

Decades ago when I read her work, I was greatly helped in recognizing how anger or depression was only a part of a progression toward a resolution of personal issues by the dying that would eventually allow them to leave this world with a settled sense of satisfaction. By making these keen observations, Dr. Kubler-Ross helped all of us to recognize that dying is a process.

Later, Dr. Kubler-Ross wrote an introduction to another work that captured national attention. Her foreword to medical doctor Raymond A. Moody's *Life After Life* added to the bestselling book's ability to spark public discussion about a scientific approach to the beyond. Moody told the stories of 50 people who had walked over the edge and come back, bringing us into new contact with the possibilities. One of Dr. Moody's contentions was that death is not the end, but a "shifting." He contended that modern science had complicated the meaning of dying by imposing definitions of death that do not really apply. In addition, his book brought, perhaps for the first time, much attention to the accounts of people who had experienced an end of life and then a return after death. Many times Christian audiences read these stories but didn't know what to say or how to react. One of the problems was that this book challenged their theological perspectives on death, and they didn't want to admit this problem out loud.

Moody's work was initiated by hearing a talk given by former U.S. Army private George Ritchie about his extraordinary experience during the Second World War. Having caught double pneumonia, Ritchie was pronounced dead and taken to the morgue. When an intern saw Ritchie's hand move, adrenaline was injected and the man's vital signs returned. Later, after becoming a psychiatrist, Dr. George Ritchie often spoke of his extraordinary spiritual encounters while he was lying in the morgue. Moody's remembrance of this talk prompted him to keep records of the stories people told after being revived. Ten years later, after becoming a medical doctor, he wrote *Life After Life*.

Other types of books began to surface, such as Betty J. Eadie's *Embraced by the Light*, and more recently Don Piper's bestselling account of his death following a terrible car collision with a truck. Written with Cecil Murphey, *90 Minutes in Heaven* tells about how one moment Piper was in this world and a moment later he knew he was in heaven. A crowd of old acquaintances stood before a shining gate, waiting to welcome him. The first person he saw was his grandfather. Don also felt the loving greeting of old friends and acquaintances. A magnificent sound of glorious music filled the air. The rest of his book is the story of his difficult and painful process of recovery after returning to his physical body.

Stages in the Process

Before *90 Minutes in Heaven* or any of the other recent near-death experience accounts were published, Kenneth Ring, Ph.D., wrote an exploration of many of the themes found in Raymond Moody's book, attempting to discover any correlations or consistencies between the stories Moody and others reported. In *Life at Death: A Scientific Investigation of the Near-Death Experience*, Ring reported that there were no parallels between gender, how a person died, social history, and the possibility of having such an experience. The near-death events appeared to occur randomly to people of all types. However, Dr. Ring did report five stages that near-death experiences often seemed to follow:

1. They entered into an out-of-body state of being. Often they could see their original bodies beside them or below them.

2. These persons immediately experienced a sensation of well-being and felt a new level of peace floating through them.

3. They had a sensation of floating into darkness, which was often like entering a tunnel or a dim void.

4. Somewhere in this travel through what might be described as "space," they had an encounter with a being, or an angel, who reviewed with them whether they should live or die. A decision was made to return and finish some work or task not yet completed.

5. After turning back, the individual met a deceased person he or she had known who told him or her that it wasn't yet time to die, and the person returned.[1]

Reviewing Ring's five stages alongside Kubler-Ross's five stages of dying provides us with a fascinating place to begin to look more deeply at our subject. Interesting enough, Moody ends his book by saying, "If experiences of the type which I have discussed are real, they have very profound implications . . . it would be true that we cannot fully understand this life until we catch a glimpse of what lies beyond it."[2]

Biblical Accounts

What appears to be common in the experience of coming up to death and then returning? Remember the original question at the beginning of this chapter about the possibility of a pattern, or a systematization, of these events? Well, before we go on, let's consider what the Bible tells us.

The Old Testament is fairly vague. In general, the deceased descended to *Sheol*, which seemed to be a rather murky place that was not well defined. The passages suggest that people were able to maintain only the faintest resemblance to their former lives. Psalm 16 promised godly hope and a possible release from this holding place for the dead:

> Therefore my heart is glad, and my glory rejoices; My flesh also will rest in hope. For You will not leave my soul in Sheol, nor will You allow Your Holy One to see corruption. You will show me the path of life; in Your presence is fullness of joy; At Your right hand are pleasures forevermore (vv. 9-11).

As the Scriptures progress, so does the writer's understanding of what can be expected on the other side of life. Perhaps, the high point of Old Testament insight comes in the book of Daniel. An apocalyptic book, the prophet Daniel strongly anticipates the coming of the Messiah. In the final chapter, he adds insight into the Jewish perspective:

> And many of those who sleep in the dust of the earth shall awake, some to everlasting life, some to shame and everlasting contempt. Those who are wise shall shine like the brightness of the firmament, and those who turn many to righteousness like the stars forever and ever (Dan. 12:2-3).

Death is analogous to sleep from which people can awake. The prophet appears to be suggesting that death is temporary and will have an end somewhere out there in the distant future. He also adds a dimension of judgment along with a promise of redemption.

Obviously, we cannot access the common attitudes of the average Jew living in the time of Daniel (sixth century B.C.). Often, what we find in Scripture is a response or recollection of a portion of what the righteous believed (as opposed to the entire belief system). Possibly, they believed more than Daniel tells us. We can't be sure.

When we turn to the New Testament, we pick up speed in a hurry. The pages are filled with stories of Jesus' healing the sick, as well as restoring life to the dead. The resurrection of Lazarus after he had been dead for three days is a landmark event (see John 11). Finally, in the crucifixion, death and resurrection, Jesus moves back and forth across the line from death to life and returning again to this world in His resurrection appearances. Yet again, it's a mysterious and wonderful occurrence that falls well outside human reason.

After Jesus' ascension, the apostle Paul developed an entire theology based on the resurrection. First Corinthians 15 is his elaborate statement on the meaning of Jesus Christ's return to life.

Later in the book, we are going to study this portion in much more detail, but we can already see that the Bible tells several near-death stories, particularly in the New Testament. But as with the other stories we've seen so far, they're still sketches that leave much to the imagination. Thankfully there is some research out there that will allow us to compare the results that have been found.

Chapter Five

Other Patterns

When Moody investigated near-death experiences and shared with the world his observations in his book, he noted that in their return, the nearly dead shared a number of common discoveries. The settings of these experiences varied significantly but the experiences often included feelings of peace, unusual noises, and seeing a dark tunnel or a dark void that might be compared to a tunnel.

What these people saw often exceeded their ability to describe the sight with earthly language. Sometimes they found themselves outside their bodies and meeting "spiritual beings," whether they were described as angels, deceased relatives or friends. Their lives sometimes flashed before their eyes. When they returned to their bodies, many found it difficult to communicate what they had seen. Afterward, their fear of death evaporated and they experienced a significant broadening of their perspective and concern for others.

Two years after the publication of his book, Moody conducted hundreds more interviews and broadened his list of common components in these experiences. Some of those components include the fact that some people seemed to find another existence where all knowledge appeared to reside. Some saw cities of light, while others reported that they witnessed a realm of confused and distraught spirits.

Raymond Moody's observations give us more fascinating evidence to explore and compare to what the Scripture indicates we should expect. With this evidence and the other data we have reviewed so far, we've seen many patterns and commonalities between the experiences and even the suggestions of the possible stages one might go through after death. Still, there is more evidence to see and more research to conduct.

Notes
1. Kenneth Ring, Ph.D., *Life at Death* (New York: Quill, 1980).
2. Raymond A. Moody, Jr., M.D., *Life After Life* (New York: Bantam Books, 1975), p. 184.

Difficult Pictures

As we review some of the difficulties with these pictures, let's remember that we are looking at brief snapshots, not a wide-screen Imax movie. This is not a continuous television documentary that we can rewind back and forth and study for hours. All we get is a quick (and often fading) picture, actually a memory, of an experience that didn't last long by a clock's standard. The spiritual adventurer may have lost all track of time and the near-death event may have felt as though it lasted for days or weeks, but usually the time was short. But because we are questing after truth, we can only work with the evidence as reported. Our goal in this section is not to make wild claims but to present solid evidence anyone can hang on to.

Since the work of Kubler-Ross, Moody and others became a topic of popular conversation, a number of objections have erupted. Individuals reported experiences that didn't fit what was then considered the "norm." Due to widely published stories of experiences, popular opinions naturally assumed certain events were expected if a near-death encounter was real. For example, many of the early accounts had talked about entering a "tunnel," and it was assumed that was where a genuine experience began for everyone. However, when the Gallup organization researched this, they found that only 9 percent of people claiming to have had an afterlife experience had ever gone through a tunnel in their adventure beyond life.[1] Such differences left some people confused and uncertain. What can we make of this?

Let's remember several things.

We're dealing with a mystery, an encounter that exceeds our human capacity for complete understanding because it is beyond our realm of personal experience. We can't talk about or describe the event in ways that make sense to people who haven't experienced it themselves because it is outside the realm of normal reason—not that the event is unreasonable or impossible to examine, but it doesn't fit the categories of syllogistic and deductive logic we normally work with. Something has occurred for which we have no basis to explore in this world.

For example, many Christians speak of the real presence of Jesus Christ in Holy Communion. They believe that in some way Jesus is present in the bread and wine, forgiving our sin and restoring us. How can Jesus Christ, born over 2,000 years ago, be present *today* in a *food* substance and a drink? Why can't we explain the connection any better? We can't explain it because it is fundamentally a *mystery*, and an event that happens beyond everyday experience.

This confusing element leads us to a second issue we should keep in mind: the limitations of language. We assume that everyone knows what we mean when we speak, but this is seldom true. Actually, we are often misunderstood because words mean different things to different people. One person may call out, "Hey, you old dog," and mean an affectionate greeting. The other person may hear, "Hey, you mangy worthless animal," and be highly offended. Happens every day.

In attempting to understand a spiritual world that no one has lived in, we must allow for a wide latitude of meaning. Seeking insight demands that we ask questions far more than it immediately assumes that we understand what's going on. When people are describing the indescribable, we must listen carefully, and pay close attention before we ask questions or make judgments.

Perspective is another very relevant ingredient. Someone may be reading what I've been written so far and say to himself, "This is nonsense." The person sitting next to him may read the same thing and say, "This is wonderful!" Why do the two readers have such vastly different perspectives?

When we begin to read or examine an issue, we usually have a particular presupposition tucked away in our minds, which will likely shift our perspective one way or another. Our prior convictions deeply affect how we see and interpret everything, especially books such as the Bible. In the same way, these presuppositions affect how we interpret near-death experiences.

The truth is that we have a multitude of convictions about everything, and these convictions shape our understanding, our personality and our opinions of this issue and that. No subject demands more openness and honest exploration than exploring the meaning of near-death experiences because no one begins in neutral. We all have our own presuppositions that need to be suspended as we consider the strange experiences we've been reading about, and those to come.

Chapter Six

Consider Mitch

Remember my father-in-law, Mitchell Brantley? In chapter 2, I wrote about his death and what followed, but there's more to the story. Let me tell you what preceded his death.

Mitch had a form of Hodgkins disease that created an aggressive cancer in his lymphatic system. During that summer, he appeared normal and responsive when his grandsons came from California for their final visit. Immediately after all the company left and the family pictures had been taken, he took a serious turn for the worse. He could still sit in his living room chair and rock but that's where things began to slide downhill.

Periodically, Mitchell would call out to his long deceased Aunt Al. Out of nowhere, he'd turn in his chair and speak to the void beside him, "Aunt Al, let me in! Please, let me in."

At first no one said anything, but with time the conversations with someone that none of us could see became more obvious and unavoidable. "Aunt Al!" Mitch would say, crying to himself, and then he would continue a conversation that was too obscure for any of us to hear.

Who was Aunt Al? None of us had ever heard the name and had no idea where this name was coming from. We thought that perhaps Mitch was hallucinating or speaking out of the effects of his disease. Our internal presuppositions and our resulting perspectives had closed our minds to the experience Mitch was in the midst of. We even tried to ignore these outbursts.

After some inquiry, I discovered that Aunt Al had been a Christian relative who had cared about Mitch when he was young. Though we couldn't prove it of course, the story surfaced that she had actually loaned Mitch money and helped him when he first started in business. Aunt Al was a person who had cared about Mitch and, as best we could tell, was standing by to help him cross the final line.

At least, that's what this brief snapshot seemed to say. But if we had relied solely on our internal presuppositions, we might have missed out on understanding this unique and rare family experience.

Cutting Through the Confusion

The first thing we must remember about these end-of-life or near-death experiences is that they differ wildly. The beginnings of these episodes are not the same for everyone, and they aren't always easy to understand or explain. Why is each experience unique to each individual? At this moment, we don't know nor do we understand how the different experiences fit the individual. When his doctor brought psychiatrist Karl Jung back from a near-death experience near the end of his life, Jung reported having found himself in an expansive library where in-depth discussions were unfolding. Jung was most unhappy about coming back to this world. Other individuals find themselves in a garden or drawn to a wondrous light. Many people do report going down a tunnel or long passageway. We don't know why the various settings are so different but we do remember Jesus saying, "in My Father's house are many mansions" (John 14:2). Could that be a reason?

Let us review several of the common similarities among beyond-life travelers. Many people report being drawn down some sort of passageway toward a light that is brighter than the sun, though it doesn't hurt the eyes. Usually a figure or several figures appear and communication seems to be telepathic, or speech without words. The dialogue seems to develop in a mental, mind-to-mind, sort of way. This very short, and likely incomplete description, gives us a prelude to the experience. In *Beyond the Light*, P. M. H. Atwater describes four different, and fairly unique, categories of near-death experiences:

1. *Initial experiences or non-experience.* More like a "seed" experience that introduces a new way to perceive reality, these encounters have ingredients of love and may include "help" voices, or voice, and a sense of out-of-body movement. However, the content is often vague or not well defined.

2. *Heaven-like experience.* Often there will be reunions with previously deceased family members as well as a review of one's past. The scene imparts reassurance and release from fear. The scenery is well defined and has a sense of place.

3. *Transcendent experience.* These encounters include revelations of higher truths and feel like entering another dimension of existence. This dimension feels more like travel to another planet or a world of different shape and magnitude.

4. *Hell-like experience.* The person enters a threatening void where his or her past feels more like a person-

al haunting. The scenes are startling and highly unpleasant. Suggestions of punishment and pain confront the individual and feel highly menacing.[2]

While this is only an observer's attempt to arrange a series of unique reports into an order, it does present us with a perspective on what may have happened to the millions who have reported such travels beyond life.

Atwater's categories also add another dimension of the evidence that we have yet to examine. So far, my reports have been of a positive variety. However, in addition to the positive, there is also a negative. When Jesus spoke about hell, He used *Gehenna*, the word for the constantly burning Jerusalem garbage dump. Matthew 5:22 reports, "Whoever says, 'You fool!' shall be in danger of hell fire." The letter of James reports the same reality (see Jas. 3:6). On this, both the Gospels and the evidence we discover in these near-death experiences agree—dimensions of both reward and punishment exist on the other side.

Complexity

Making sense out of snapshots of these complex and intriguing mysteries can be demanding work. This subject will stretch us, open our minds and even prove frightening to some people. You might be asking yourself, *Why should I put myself through this exercise?* The answer is, because what you learn might change the most frightening inevitability of your life into the most overpowering promise you could ever imagine.

Chapter Six

Notes
1. George Gallup, *Adventures in Immortality* (New York: McGraw Hill, 1982).
2. P. M. H. Atwater, *Beyond the Light: The Mysteries and Revelations of Near-Death Experiences* (New York: Avon Books, 1995).

The Children

While living in Laguna Beach, California, I worked with a new congregation near the ocean. One of the members served as a nurse in Fullerton, working in a hospital unit that treated children with terminal cancers and similar deadly diseases. Mary Allison had a hard job. While I admired her consistent concern for the sick, I certainly wouldn't have wanted her job.

One spring morning I received an urgent phone call from Mary. "Robert, I know you speak Spanish and I need you to come at once."

"What's happened?" I asked her.

"We've got a five-year-old child dying of cancer. She can't speak English and neither do her parents. We're desperate to understand what's going on. Please come and help us translate."

"I'll be right there," I assured Mary. "I'm on my way."

When I got to the hospital, I discovered that the family had wandered in from somewhere in the south of New Mexico or Arizona. The little girl, Alicia, had been receiving chemotherapy but was losing ground. The nurses said she'd lost her hair and the bumps covering her body were cancers pushing to the surface. No one could do anything and the child would soon die. They wanted me to attempt to make some sense out of what she was feeling.

I slipped into Alicia's room and found her sleeping. Just as I had been told, this beautiful little girl had lost all her hair. Across her arms, legs and chest, I could see the telltale tumors that had pressed up under her skin. Her mother and father huddled together in the corner of the room with a look of terror on their faces.

"*Como esta ustedes,*" I began.

The mother shook her head. "*No bien,*" she lamented.

I tried to understand their history but it was difficult. Eventually I concluded that they spoke a dialect that was somewhat like the Tarahumara Indians of a remote area of Northern Mexico. They seemed to have come from somewhere south or maybe west of Nogales in the Sonora area. Their speech was an amalgamation of this dialect with some Spanish and English mixed in. They seemed to be nice people who had wandered into the United States looking for work. Somehow or the other, they had ended up in Los Angeles and they got by the best they could.

When Alicia awoke, I was surprised that her Spanish was much better and more easy to understand. Somewhere along the way she had become more cultured than her parents and had learned the Spanish language well. The child began speaking to me intently. She understood that her life was about to end and she was trying to comfort her parents. Reversing the child-adult roles, Alicia had actually become their source of solace and she didn't want to tell them how overwhelming her pain actually was. Often this happens with children when the parents fall apart.

Alicia told me that her entire body ached. I squeezed her hand and asked her if she had ever been in a church. Alicia said she had no idea what a church was. The five-year-old child had never heard the Christian story and had no idea who Jesus was.

For several moments I talked with her about the love of God and how Jesus the Christ had come to set us free from the fear of death. Alicia listened intently and nodded her head knowingly. She seemed quite accepting of what I was saying. Finally, she told me that she wished to go back to sleep because the land of her dreams was so much more pleasant than this world.

"What do you see when you are asleep?" I asked her.

"Oh, I see beautiful creatures!" For the first time Alicia's eyes brightened. "They seem to be flying all around and over my bed."

"Really!" My consternation turned toward fascination with what Alicia was saying. The child had never heard of angels and yet she was clearly describing a Christian concept.

"They fly around me and are very, very pretty," Alicia said. "Then there's a man who stands by. He's my friend."

"What is his name?" I asked.

Alicia looked puzzled, "I don't know. I never ask him but I know he's my friend."

"I think his name might be Jesus," I said. "Next time you dream, call him Jesus and see what happens. And I believe what you are seeing flying above you are called angels."

Alicia nodded and went to sleep.

Her parents' grief was so heavy that it was impossible to comfort them while not understanding their native language. Both the father and mother huddled together, hugging each other and crying. I sat there feeling feeble, trying to help, all the while praying that God would intervene in some way.

An hour later, Alicia woke up again. She beckoned for me to come near so that she could whisper in my ear.

"I talked to Jesus," she said. "He's so kind. He told me this was the last time that I had to come back. Next time I go to sleep, I can go home with him. He's going to take care of me."

"Wonderful," I said without really understanding what I was saying.

"Yes," Alicia said. "This time is almost over," she said with unexpected maturity and pressed my hand. "I want to go to sleep now."

The child rolled over and in a few minutes she was gone.

In the midst of her staggering pain, Alicia's was one of the most peaceful deaths I have ever observed.

Forbid Them Not

Did I know what I was doing standing by Alicia's bed? Not in the least!

I walked into a situation for which I had no preparation and could only deal with it step by step as it unfolded. Actually, I wasn't as bewildered as the parents but I wasn't far from it by the time Alicia died. Much of the time, we learn by jumping in when something needs to be done and then later reflect on what we've seen. In this case, there were several important things that Alicia taught me.

First of all, Alicia didn't close her eyes hoping to wake up at some future date after some apocalyptic event had occurred. Alicia was in this world one minute and then gone to another realm that we might call heaven seconds later. However that fits with your theology, it is what I observed. The swiftness of the transition gives us something to ponder. In addition, while Alicia had not been trained in a Christian environment or brought up around the church, the realities of heaven had somehow opened up for her. It only took a little nudging from me to help her name and identify what she was experiencing, but it all fit together. Another observation: I sensed that Alicia demonstrated intelligence and maturity far beyond her years. Her language became more adult as her death approached. Finally, she left this world without fear or apprehension.

Jesus said, "Let the little children come to Me, and do not forbid them; for such is the kingdom of God" (Mark 10:14) and this seems to fit Alicia's situation. Obviously, near-death experiences aren't reserved only for adults.

One of the first professional examinations of children's near-death experiences came in Dr. Melvin Morse's book *Closer to the Light: Learning from the Near-Death Experiences of Children*.[1] A pediatrician, Dr. Morse became intrigued when a patient who nearly drowned came back after spending three days in a coma, and then told amazing stories of a wonderful journey she had taken while everyone else thought she was dying. After Morse's book came out, other medical personnel began making similar discoveries. Often, these stories were so amazing that even atheistic doctors and agnostic nurses changed their minds about death and the afterlife. They were touched by their patients' stories and recognized that they had overlooked a crucial dimension of life, and death.

One of Dr. Morse's observations was that children, like adults, seem to be greeted on the other side by a welcoming person. The "greeter" may possibly be a relative or individual they had known in the past. It appeared to be the role of this greeter to settle any fears and put them in touch with someone familiar. Dr. Morse also found that 70 percent of children with near-death experiences encountered angels, which was the case for Alicia.

Researchers who have worked in this area have also noted that child "experiencers" come back with a deep interest in the Church. Their commitment to a religious faith is profoundly deepened, and after such an experience they generally take religious matters more seriously. Often, children create some form of worship center in their bedrooms and may read the Bible zealously.

What Can We Say?

The evidence from my own personal experience and from professional studies like that of Dr. Morse is that children are as much a part of this process as their parents. Once they have stepped over the line, the step proves to be a giant leap affecting their expectations, sensitivities and behavior upon their return. We find that putting one's ear into eternity changes what we hear for the rest of our lives, and children are no exception.

Note

1. Melvin Morse, M.D., with Paul Perry, *Closer to the Light: Learning from the Near-Death Experiences of Children* (New York: Villard Books, 1992).

The Dark Side

Most of the near-death experiences I have studied are positive, with individuals finding new purpose and the sense of a divine mission in their lives. These folks offer hope to the rest of us and relate that they are no longer afraid of death. However, the question very quickly arises, Are there any negative encounters? Does anyone come back in complete despair? Does anybody see blackness? Is there anything frightening out there?

Sorry, but the answer is unequivocally yes.

While working on this book, I interviewed many professionals who worked with the dying. Some were doctors, some were nurses and others were pastors or chaplains. Several hospice organizations provided me with a list of a significant number of clergy who pray with the dying on a daily basis. They have many stories to tell, but some are not so hopeful.

Reverend Ray Wade worked as a chaplain with Preferred Hospice in Oklahoma City, Oklahoma, and while he did he observed the downside of death. A sensitive man with a heart for helping the dying slip across the final line as easily as possible, Ray recalled working with a woman who had struggled with the disease of alcoholism during much of her lifetime. She was often angry and responded to Ray most of the time with violent and non-verbal responses emanating hostility. Like having delirium tremens (often called the D.T.s), even though she no longer touched alcohol in any form, the woman kept slapping at imaginary bugs and remained agitated much of the time as her body slowly gave out. In contrast to other people's more peaceful experiences of talking to relatives or friends who had died in the past, this woman maintained a constant fear of someone that only she could see who stood in the corner of the room. She appeared to know and recognize the invisible figure and remained apprehensive up to the final moment of her life in this world. The woman seemed to see beyond the edge of life, but what she saw was not a pretty sight.

Is There a Hell?

The Christian faith records Jesus' teaching clearly about both heaven and hell. In fact, you might be surprised to discover that Jesus actually talked more about hell than He did about heaven. In our contemporary secularist society, we don't often talk about this dimension of the Bible's teaching. Most churches today might not even have a sermon on the subject in their entire history. Teaching about a final judgment of any sort might be considered too negative and likely to scare off visitors. Consequently, the teaching about hell drops through the cracks in the church floor.

But what does the Bible teach?

Scripture maintains that there will be a final judgment. Hebrews 9:27 proclaims, "as it is appointed for men to die once, but after this the judgment, so Christ was offered once to bear the sins of many. To those who eagerly wait for Him He will appear a second time."

The fact of a final accounting is a significant part of the New Testament's teaching. Whether one understands these passages to be metaphor or fact, hell is described as a place of darkness that is full of weeping and gnashing of teeth; it is also described as a fiery furnace. The New Testament is strikingly clear in its diagnosis of an ultimate judgment on the human condition.

Anglican theologian J. I. Packer believes and teaches that the lost will be confronted with four realities in hell. First, they will be forced to recognize that their life on Earth was lived in a manner that is repulsive in their Creator's sight. Second, they will discover that their exclusion from God's realm of righteousness and joy was correct. Third, they will continually face the fact that all their hope and pleasure is gone forever. Fourth, the lost will be confronted with the fact that their condition will forever remain unchangeable.[1] While some believers might disagree with Packer's assessment, it is true that his teaching accurately reflects the Scriptures.

The issue of salvation turns on encountering Jesus Christ, through a personal, intimate relationship with the one true God. This connection between the individual and the Almighty is the key that unlocks the door to heaven. The matter is expressed clearly in the most well-known verses in the Bible. John 3:16-17 proclaims, "For God so loved the world that he gave his only begotten Son, that whoever believes in Him should not perish but have everlasting life. For God did not send His Son into the world to condemn the world, but that the world through Him might be saved."

In this context, the Greek word *pisteuon*, derived from the word *pisteus*, means "believing" and implies far more that the mental acceptance of a fact. Belief demands placing one's life entirely behind the faith required to walk with Christ. In this way, conviction and ethics go hand in hand into eternity, and this clearly seems to be a part of the biblical picture of what's "out there."

A Look at the Dark Side

Different researchers have reported people describing a descent rather than an ascent during their near-death experience. Gracia Ellwood, a researcher, found that Gloria Hipple had such an event. A native of Blakeslee, Pennsylvania, Gloria had serious complications after a miscarriage, and during the time she was struggling with serious bleeding, Gloria lapsed into a black episode.

She remembered being pulled downward into a spinning vortex. While she couldn't tell what was happening, Gloria knew her body was plunging headfirst downward into the darkness. She tried to grab the sides of the vortex but nothing would stop her fall. Gloria remembered thinking about her children and being distraught over who might care for them. She kept screaming out for help for their sake but nothing stopped her downward fall. Gloria could only identify that the cyclonic void appeared to taper into a funnel. At the other end, she saw a black spot that grew even darker than the funnel. The dot enlarged into a black curtain. However, as she got closer she saw a white dot that appeared like a bright light at the end of the funnel. Maybe, she was on her way out of the funnel.

Unfortunately, the white dot turned out to be a small white skull. As Gloria came closer, the skull grew in size and morphed into a leering, grinning face with bare eye sockets. The gaping mouth hung open as the skull flew at her like a careening baseball. Gloria was both terrified for herself and for the fate of her children. She kept screaming out her concern for the well-being of her children. Suddenly, the skull shattered into fragments and her drop slowed. A great white light replaced the skull and became a welcoming, calming light. Gloria began to sense herself floating upward and could hear her husband calling her name. She realized that she could open her eyes and suddenly found herself back in the hospital room.[2]

While Gloria Hipple's experience doesn't fit the typical expectations of hell, the imagery of her experience is still significantly frightening. She called it the most horrendous experience of her life, yet found it to be gratifying at the same time because she received a second chance in which she might improve herself.

Some people do confront demons or devilish figures, just as others have positively reported seeing angels. Some people describe torture chambers or black rooms where pain was inflicted. A young man named Scott had an encounter that comes closer to the usual expectations.

Scott was crossing the street with his mother to buy an ice cream cone from a vendor when a car struck him, sending him somersaulting through the air and landing 25 feet away on the pavement. Scott suddenly found himself watching the accident from up in a nearby tree. He quickly realized that no one could hear him talk and that he was cut off from his mother. In his next memory he was in a dark place and flying through a black tunnel with the feeling that he was both floating and being propelled by a wind of some sort. While traveling through the tunnel, Scott found himself face to face with a demon or the devil and was severely frightened.

Rather than the usual description of a demon or of the devil that surfaces at Halloween, complete with pitchfork and horns, the Evil One in Scott's experience appeared as a large mass of rotting flesh. This malevolent entity responded to Scott in both a sick and crazy way filled with anger. This entity kept telling Scott that he was bad and was now trapped under the Devil's control. Terrified in this dark place, Scott remembered crossing a room and finding his uncle who had died two years earlier, and he was still covered by the same sheet or blanket used when the man died of cancer. During this time, Scott recalled that they conversed telepathically.

Then shortly after encountering his uncle, Scott was escorted out of the realm of darkness and woke up in a hospital room several hours after the accident. While recovering from his injuries, Scott remained plagued by nightmares about his horrific experience with the devilish figure he had seen. He was left with an absolute conviction that he never again wanted to meet this evil creature, and as a result, he resolved to become closer to God.[3]

The Reality of Hell

At this stop in our journey, we can again observe that the stories of people who have experienced dark places beyond the boundary of death fit with biblical expectations. At the very least, the evidence shows that near-death encounters do not contradict scriptural expectations. We have detailed records of people experiencing both the best and the worst.

Cardiologist Maurice Rawlings discovered that his patients tended to repress anything negative that came through after a near-death experience. However, he reported in his book *Beyond Death's Door* that nearly half the people he interviewed after resuscitation described experiences that sounded like they came from a place that sounded like hell.[4] If this is correct, then the number may be larger than we have suspected.

As was true of those who enter heaven, these people who experienced some measure of darkness, some measure of hell, were better for having had the experience. Like Scott, the horrifying afterlife trip changed many of their perspectives, their behaviors and their lives drastically.

Notes

1. J. I. Packer, foreword to Ajith Fernando, *Crucial Questions About Hell* (Wheaton, IL: Crossway Books, 1991,) p. x.
2. P. M. H. Atwater, *The Complete Idiot's Guide to Near-Death Experiences* (New York: Alpha Books, 2000), pp. 32-33.
3. Ibid., p. 31.
4. Maurice Rawlings, M.D., *Beyond Death's Door* (Nashville, TN, Thomas Nelson Publishers, 1978).

Learning from the Pictures

Those who wait on the LORD shall renew their strength; they shall
mount up with wings like eagles, they shall run and not be weary,
they shall walk and not faint.

ISAIAH 40:31

The dead don't die. They look on and help.

D. H. LAWRENCE

ENGLISH NOVELIST AND POET

In the second section, we will review the objections that arise
about the veracity of the evidence, and we will also see what we
can learn or deduce from the patterns and similarities of these
experiences. We will consider several concepts that influence
how we interpret the words of the dying, such as perception
and symbolism. Finally, after interviewing dozens of witnesses,
talking to many near-death experiencers and reading dozens of
sources on the subject, I have compiled the Seven Final Steps
the dying most commonly experience, a list that I hope will
offer assurance and expectancy for what is beyond.

Addressing Objections

Don Piper is a Baptist minister. In l989, he died in a car wreck.

Several years later, Rev. Piper and Cecil Murphey wrote the story of what happened *after* his sudden and untimely death.

His bestselling story paints a picture of what occurred when Don was driving home from a church conference held at Trinity Pines on the north shore of Lake Livingston near Houston, Texas.[1] Driving his red 1986 Ford Escort, he intended to travel down the Gulf Freeway and chose to take a narrow road that crossed a section of Lake Livingston, developed from damming a portion of the Trinity River. The bridge was narrow and looked dangerous. At 50 miles an hour, Don believed he shouldn't have any problems. Unfortunately, an 18-wheel semi-truck entered the bridge from the other side.

Driven by an employee of the Texas Department of Corrections, the truck veered over the center line and smashed head-on into Piper's Ford. Moving at 60 miles an hour, the truck roared over the top of the Ford and smashed it with an impact equal to hitting a tree at 110 miles per hour. The only thing that kept Don's car from flying off into the lake was a sturdy bridge railing, but the head-on collision was enough to finish him off. Rev. Piper died instantly.

The next thing Piper realized, he was standing in heaven. Large iridescent gates stood before him and a crowd of people rushed forward to greet him. One quick glance told Don that these were people who had all died earlier. Out of the crowd, his grandfather Joe Kulbeth stepped out to welcome him with a big, warm hug. In this large greeting committee stood one of his high school friends who had been an outstanding athlete but who had died in a car wreck at the age of 19 years old. When he looked around, Don realized that the people standing around him had each shared a role helping him to become a strong and growing Christian.

Wondrous light bathed the scene. Eventually, the crowd started moving toward the source of that great light. As he moved with the crowd toward the center of the light that Don believed was God, he felt a holy awe fill him and then he started to hear magnificent music. In Don's recollections of this experience, he remembers the amazing feeling of being surrounded by love. Never had he heard such moving sounds. Like worship music arising from a cathedral choir, the songs were filled with praise and joy. Much of the music blessed Jesus as the Christ who had become the King of kings. Piper found himself filled with the deepest sense of well-being and belonging, and he was ready to stay forever.

In the next moment, everything changed. Just as suddenly as he had come, Don Piper left heaven.

The emergency medical technicians pronounced him dead as soon as they arrived because he had died instantly when the wreck occurred at 11:45 in the morning. It was not until 1:15 P.M. that they decided to move the body. To the EMTs' surprise, they discovered that Don had a pulse. Although his body was mangled and it would take months before he was mobile again, Don Piper had come back to share his time in heaven.

As Don's book *90 Minutes in Heaven* comes to a close, Piper asks, "What did God want me to learn from all my experiences, my death, and the long period of recovery? How can my experiences be of the most benefit to others?"[2]

We can ask ourselves these two questions after reading the stories, experiences and research about near death and the afterlife contained in this book. What can you and I learn from these experiences, and how can this new knowledge benefit those around us? Let's consider these questions as we go forward.

The Medical Explanation

Unfortunately, a number of people regard these experiences with outright skepticism and disdain. Before we go further, let's pause and consider how medical science might explain what happened to Don Piper. How does the scientific world already respond to these amazing experiences and reports of so many millions of people? We can't skirt the issue of hard objections and, in fact, I believe we must face them head on. There are skeptics standing on the sidelines and we must listen to their protests if we are going to be credible. In the following paragraphs, we will address three ways that medicine or science might explain the experience of someone like Don Piper.

1. It's All in Your Head
On January 20, 1999, Dean Eddell, M.D., responded to experiences like Rev. Don Piper's and declared that no matter how exciting they may sound, they are essentially the product of

oxygen deprivation. His professional opinion was that these experiences are nothing more than a result of a physical response to this condition.

Hypoxia in its severest form is a critical loss of oxygen and can produce visual distortions that sound significantly like near-death experiences. Often, scientifically measured experiences can produce out-of-body sensations like the feeling of floating or seeing bright lights. Therefore, doctors like Dean Eddell point to hypoxia as an explanation.

Is it possible? Absolutely, and the evidence is out there to support Dr. Eddell's theory. However, Don Piper and others would likely point out that they did not experience oxygen deprivation during the car wreck.

Some professionals maintain that a decrease in oxygen produces many of the experiences that seem to occur widely at the time of near-death. They suggest that seeing lights or going down long tunnels comes from the effect that a lack of oxygen has on the brain. Once oxygen is restored as the person regains vitality, the strange experiences subside and disappear. In the same way, it is theorized that electrical shock can produce unusual effects, such as hearing unexpected music.

For many of the experiences we have reviewed so far, including Piper's and that of Jack Oscar and J. B. Phillips, oxygen deprivation wasn't a part of the situation at all, thereby negating this possibility. Let's move on to the next potential medical cause.

2. It's in Your Stomach

Another approach for explaining how the afterlife events happen is to suggest that the experiencers took some kind of drug that sent their brains spinning off into hallucinations. Professionals suggest that drugs in some form might have been used for getting high and, as a result, weird events happened in the minds of some of these people. Generally used as an anesthetic, Ketamine is known to produce strange effects. Many of the characteristics of the experiences of the nearly-dead, such as visions of lights or going down a long, shrouded pathway as well as contact with "other beings," have resulted with Ketamine. Therefore, some professionals may point to such a drug as the reason for the encounters with the beyond.

Of course, LSD, marijuana and other similar hallucinogenic substances also produce experiences that sound amazingly close to what people say they encountered when they stepped over the line. Another avenue that has been considered is what happens when the body produces endorphins, which is short for the medical term endogenous morphine. These self-produced chemicals are the body's method of reacting to pain by producing its own inner responses that bring relief. Some medical doctors have pointed toward this type of chemical as the reason for out-of-body experiences.

It is safe to assume that five-year-old Alicia wasn't using LSD before she died, and the same is true of Piper, Phillips and many of the others we have reviewed so far, but of course you never know for sure.

3. It's in Your Imagination

Some say that as part of the self-preservation mechanism inside each of us, as we are dying, our brains go into a kind of self-protective mode. The deteriorating brain surrounds the individual with feelings that are comforting, which might result in seeing an unusual light or the faces of old friends, but it's theorized that this is only our imaginations at work. In an attempt to give a scientific view of near-death events, Susan Blackmore developed detailed theories of how the brain might produce such results. She believes anoxia might cause the sound of music by stimulating the cochlear region of the ear. Endorphins and neurotransmitters can cause the hippocampus area of the brain to bring memories to mind that could produce a movie-like survey of one's entire life. Feelings of timelessness might result from the breakup of the personality as death approaches. Ms. Blackmore's theories are complex, but in simplest terms they all suggest that these unusual events happen only in the imagination.[3]

Some professionals have suggested other ideas associated with imagination, such as the ideas that fantasy-prone personalities might be more apt to produce a near-death kind of experience. Such persons have a predisposition toward the hysterical end of the psychological scale and sometimes come up with far-out imaginary ideas of every sort. The suggestion would be that such persons simply make up these stories.

Could people make up such a fantastic story? Richard Selzer, M.D., wrote *Raising the Dead: A Doctor's Encounter with His Own Mortality* to fabricate exactly that sort of story. After the book was in the marketplace, Selzer admitted that he only wanted "to tell a ripping good story." I'm sure that there are people who do this after hearing about near-death experiences, but because I was standing there with Mitch Brantley during his experience and death, and Cindi Pursely worked with patients like Betty Meier and Al Harris before they died, I'm afraid that this doesn't fit our experiences with near-death.

Beyond the Objections

I'd be among the first to recognize that conditions like hypoxia can produce unusual effects. Sure, oxygen deprivation can cause the mind to do flip-flops. Moreover, we live in a drug-infested culture and nation. Only the most uninformed and naive person would not admit that hallucinations can happen to anyone who ingests psychedelic drugs. Yes, the Dr. Eddells of the world are correct when they talk about the effects of oxygen deprivation or stimulation. However, these explanations simply don't fit the majority of the situations and experiences we have reviewed. There are millions of near-death experiences that simply could not have been caused by one of the aforementioned explanations. So what do we do when science can't explain everything?

My conclusion is that we're talking about two different worlds.

Some of the medical community shares a common viewpoint of attempting to explain all seemingly supernatural experience by physical explanation. Ever since the Enlightenment (beginning around A.D. 1500), society has had a preference for science rather than religion or faith in explaining how the world works. Some scientists seem to view strange or hard-to-explain experiences as magic tricks. There's a simple, rational, medical explanation and their job is to find it. Like demonstrating how the handkerchief disappears up the magician's sleeve, they believe a chemical, physical or biological answer will reveal the truth about what's really going on *in every circumstance*. While science has been extremely important in helping us to better understand the world and put away false superstitions, the field still has its limitations. Science can't take us into the spiritual realm.

While dying obviously has physical dimensions, the process also blurs the lines between this world and the one beyond. The physical and the spiritual realms meet and overlap as a person is slipping away. In this process of transition, the dying person seems to have a foot in each world as he or she crosses over from this world into eternity. Science can't make that journey with that person. As far as we can tell, the reach of test tubes and stethoscopes ends when the heart stops beating. We can analyze why a person died but we can't tell where he or she has gone. The mystery is as great today as it was when the pharaohs built pyramids thousands of years ago. The experience of dying forces us to respect the dividing line between our world and the ultimate frontier.

On the other hand, a reader might be saying, "Wait a minute! I've never seen *any* of these effects you are describing with people I know or have seen die." I understand this reluctance because I've walked with many pastors who have not experienced these occurrences throughout their entire ministries. Sometimes they shake their heads, unsure of how to handle this great mystery of life.

I think that the reason we don't hear more about near-death experiences or reports of an afterlife is due to several factors. Fieldwork seems to indicate that many people slip immediately into a coma before death, or their moment of death is unforeseen and immediate, as by a tragic accident. In these situations, there is often no time or opportunity to observe anything except the heart stopping. Unquestionably, more people die in this way than any other. I've also found that death can be a very private experience. A patient may seem to wait until the loved ones are gone from the room before he or she expires. While this may seem strange to us, it happens often enough that it doesn't seem to be a coincidence. If we are not around many deaths, that may be our experience with someone close to us. In addition, people may not call a pastor until the end is at hand. Delays like this limit observation time as well.

The same is true for doctors. Often, physicians do their work and then turn to other patients waiting on them. They may be summoned to examine the patients *after* death has occurred. Under those circumstances, they are not likely to see the final hours or minutes of the patient before death. The fact that many doctors haven't seen these experiences reflects the nature of their practice more than it does their time with patients.

However, it is interesting to note that Dr. Raymond Moody helped begin modern consideration of the subject of near-death experiences out of his own medical practice. The experiences of Dr. George Ritchie, who was a psychiatrist, stimulated Moody's inquiries. Dr. Elisabeth Kubler-Ross developed her theories out of her own medical practice as well. There are physicians out there who have seen these events and learn to pay attention, and then try to understand them.

Is there an explanation for the occurrences in these amazing end-of-life events? I believe there is, but we won't find them in a medical text or book of science. We must turn to the Bible.

Pressing On

Don Piper came out of his terrible car crash in a wrecked physical condition. His body had been ripped apart and he spent months lying in a hospital room wearing an Ilizarov growth device on his leg to allow for healing. His recovery spun on into years of pain that required Don to overcome agonizing difficulties. Even though he experienced great joy in heaven, he returned to experience great suffering on Earth. Yet, Don's sharing his story touched countless numbers of people struggling with the faith and belief issues. His experience in heaven was so remarkable that he continues to long to return and yet he knows that he is serving a purpose here in this world that has helped other strugglers travel on.

Notes

1. Don Piper with Cecil Murphey, *90 Minutes in Heaven* (Grand Rapids, MI: Revell, 2004).
2. Ibid.
3. Susan Blackmore, *Dying to Live: Science and Near-Death Experience* (New York: HarperCollins, 1993).

What Can We Learn?

My youngest son, Tate, was 15 years old when we moved to Oklahoma City from Lake Forest, California. He found a new friend across the street named John Faulk. Even though it was 30 years ago, I can still remember John sitting on Tate's bed talking and wearing a pair of cowboy boots. A happy, friendly kid, John was the type of boy that a parent wants his son to know. His father was a minister and the Faulk family included a brother, Colby, and a sister named Delila. George and Carol Faulk maintained a fine home and kept a careful eye on the children. I was pleased Tate had found such a good buddy who lived right across the street.

During the summer, Tate went off to the church camp like he did every year and came back on Friday night. I had planned to pick him up in the church parking lot as usual and hear his exciting stories of what had happened while adventuring through the wilds of church camp. Sounded like a good way to finish off Tate's summer vacation. But I didn't expect what happened on Thursday night.

The full story didn't drift through our house until early Friday morning. Apparently, John Faulk went swimming late Thursday afternoon in another friend's pool not far away. As best as anyone could tell, John had been swimming when something happened. Later, medical tests discovered it was a heart attack. Tate's best friend died in that swimming pool.

Of course, grief overwhelmed our entire family and John's death filled us with anguish. I waited until Tate returned on Friday evening before I went over to the Faulks' home to express our condolences. I knew that Tate would want to be with me. When I picked him up at the church and told him the news, Tate could hardly speak. With deepest apprehension, we drove over to the Faulks' house to express our laments.

George met us at the door and ushered us in. To my surprise, John's father seemed more composed than I expected. We sat down to talk but what George had to say was more than I could have anticipated.

"I think you'll understand what happened last night," George said. "But we're not telling everyone this story because some people wouldn't understand."

"Yes," I answered with uncertainty.

"We couldn't go to bed until late . . . probably one or two o'clock," George said. "We were so torn up that nothing made any sense. Finally, we lay down and only hoped we could go to sleep. I was almost dozing when I realized someone was standing at the end of the bed. It was almost like being in a dream, but I looked up and *there was John*."

I saw Tate's eyes widen and his mouth drop slightly. Not sure of how to respond, I waited for George to continue.

"John spoke to me almost telepathically," George said. "I'm not sure any words were said that my eardrums would have picked up but he was certainly communicating with me. He told me that there was an important reason in God's plan for why he had died. I couldn't understand it because it was too complicated for a person in this world to grasp, but he had been called into eternity because there was a role that he had to play there. John told me that he had been allowed the unusual privilege of coming back and talking to us before he went 'over.' Those were the words that he used, saying that there was an area that he had to cross over to get to the other side."

I carefully listened to George talk, and watched his face. I wondered if he was hallucinating or manufacturing a story that comforted him, but I found no hint of delusion or self-deception. George wasn't weeping and didn't looking distraught. His story was related as factually as if he were telling me the news from the morning paper. He recounted John's midnight visit as calmly as relating a story about the boy coming home from football practice.

"I have a new friend who is going to help me cross over," John had told his father as he stood at his bedside the night before. "You don't know him, but George Morgan died in Oklahoma City last year. He was a young man and helps people like me get across now. Don't worry, Dad. I'm fine."

With those words John Faulk left his family and this world behind. Suddenly, he was gone as quickly as he had come into the Faulks' bedroom. George Faulk later traced the facts in John's story and indeed found that a young man named George Morgan had died the year before in Oklahoma City.

Communications of Assurance

George Faulk had been a minister for years when John died and, of course, he believed in heaven and the Bible, had preached at funerals, and maintained the promises of Scripture. But the death of a son or daughter is the worst calamity anyone can endure. Years go by and the pain remains as fresh as the day the child died. Everything that George had proclaimed from the pulpit was challenged by the totally unexpected demise of his beloved child. *But* what did he hang on to when his son died? What was it that gave him lasting assurance about the fate of his child?

When John came back to tell his father that a plan was in place for everything that had happened, George found hope that John's death was not a quirk of fate but a strand in a divine tapestry that stretched beyond all of the tomorrows to come. The son had an important lesson to impart to the father. The lesson was that there was a divine plan for the events that had occurred, that George could trust God with his son. While the divine order was painful, when George heard John explain why he had to leave, the plan sounded magnificent in its scope and design. John returned to assure his father and mother not to worry and mourn because the hand of God held all things. John's parents could hang on to that promise.

Then, a year later, that contract was put to the ultimate test. While climbing a rope at school, Colby Faulk tumbled over on the gym floor and also died of a heart attack. Once again, the story of the severe loss surged through the neighborhood. Everyone realized that the Faulk family was being pushed to the edge of all human endurance. How could anyone go on under such circumstances? In fact, the Faulks not only went on but they also started the work of Compassionate Friends in Oklahoma City. The members of this unusual group have all lost children and support each other with love and care that can only be given by friends who know personally how deep such a loss can go. A number of times I have spoken to Compassionate Friends and have attempted to encourage the struggling members. Each of these visits reminds me of Colby and John and the lesson learned—that God has a plan at work behind all of these tragedies.

Because death has forever been such a taboo subject in our society, we rarely inquire about what the dying might be able to communicate. The idea that the almost-departed can teach us anything seems preposterous, and yet the evidence is everywhere. Whether they are aware of their pedagogical role or not, the dying can help us better prepare for the inevitable moment when all of us must cross that line.

And did you notice that the father and son roles were reversed in George and John's story? As was true in the case of little Alicia, somehow a kind of maturity was imparted during these final moments. Greater intelligence and competency appears to have been acquired and these children in their unexpected deaths became people of phenomenal insight. They are leaving behind their extraordinary discoveries for anyone who will notice.

Examining the Similarities

There is another equally notable fact about these stories. If the individuals are hallucinating, they are all delusional *in the same ways*, the likelihood of which is very low, if these stories are just hallucinations. Having worked with people struggling with alcohol and drug addiction, I quickly recognized how unusual this is. People high on psychedelics see weird images but they are rarely similar in form or content. When people are ill and have high temperatures, their hallucinations *are always wildly different.* The picture that emerges from these experiences of the dying *are remarkably alike,* and these similarities in what the nearly-dead experience adds another dimension for us to think about. Let's take a closer look at the similarities and see what we might discover.

While the initial settings or locations may vary when individuals describe their experiences, there are striking consistencies. Some people find themselves in a room or met by a group of former friends while others are surrounded by light or stand before a magnificent gate. When Dr. Raymond Moody did the research for *Life After Life,* he actually identified 15 common ingredients in his patients' encounters, despite all the unique locations and settings. Two years later after more research, Moody added four more common components, some of which will sound like other research we reviewed. Some of the results he found included the following consistent experiences:

- Seeing a long dim tunnel
- Walking into or toward a light
- Experiencing an out-of-body experience
- Meeting spiritual beings of some order, such as angels
- Doing some kind of life review
- Seeing a city of light or a place of frightened or disoriented spirits
- Finding a world where all knowledge resides
- Knowing the apparent elimination of the fear of death

- Receiving information about why the person is returning
- Returning to the body

Now a tunnel certainly doesn't occur in every near-death experience, but a sense of personal presence or meeting with someone seems to be universal. Information is almost always imparted, which usually includes some clarification of why the person is being returned to his former life. When these persons return, they come back with a drastically changed perspective.

We've seen some similar research in a previous chapter, but let's take something from Moody's observations. These common experiences came from a wide group of diverse people and occur with a kind of uncanny predictability, which is highly inconsistent with what happens in a situation of high fever, oxygen deprivation, drugs or imaginary fantasies. The simple fact that these similarities exist is enough to cause us to question the basic medical conclusions.

The Larger Lesson

On December 20, 2005, Barbara Walters presented a special entitled *Where Is Heaven?* on the ABC television network. This particular hour-long show investigated the idea of eternal life and what form it might take. The program began by mentioning that 90 percent of the American public believes in heaven. That figure means that 9 out of 10 citizens hold a firm conviction that there is an afterlife and they hope to be part of eternity.

During the documentary, Walters explored various ideas about heaven and investigated a number of near-death experiences. Her discovery was that these experiences changed the dying people's perception of themselves and of death. Judgmental attitudes tended to evaporate. Although she tried to maintain a neutral position, Ms. Walters seemed to lean toward affirming that these near-death experiences were valid.

However, the fascinating main point of the special became clear as the program progressed. The proposition that the program promoted was that *things don't end at death; they only change.* In heaven, love, peace and happiness become visible and we see them. Certainly, this suggestion rings true with John Faulk's return after his death. *John died but his spirit's existence didn't end; his spirit only changed* (see 1 Cor. 15:51-52).

Perhaps, this is another lesson to take home with us. Is the idea Christian? You bet!

Reading the Pictures

Occasionally a good mystery novel will come along in which the plot hinges on a character's discovering an unexpected insight by looking at a photograph. The picture has been there all the time but finally this individual recognizes a surprise clue that exposes the "bad guy" in the tale. A good, critical second look makes sense out of the mystery. Another way to say this is, *Perception can change what we see in a picture.*

Everyone has seen trick pictures, such as a black and white print that can be seen either as a goblet or as two faces turned in profile. In other pictures, the shadows seem to be an abstract design, but after careful study, the shadows form the shape of a person. The point is that people often look at pictures and miss something critical that makes all the difference in what they understand is happening. Again, *the issue is perception*, or how you look at the picture.

I've found that many people tend to discount details while a friend or loved one is dying. They don't watch closely or listen intently. Then, abruptly the passing is over. They usually become so busy with funeral preparations that they dismiss the unusual details of the situation. If we let these experiences slide away, we lose the lessons the dying can teach us. Often, we need to go back and take another look at the "pictures."

Here's a picture worth remembering.

Meet Von Owen

Von Owen was the father of one of my dearest friends and fellow clergyman Michael Owen. For years we worked together in the Communion of Evangelical Episcopal Churches. Seldom have I witnessed such a close and personal relationship between a father and son as I observed between Von and Michael Owen. Mike's parents Von and Judy were special people to all who knew them. Because Michael and I had worked so closely in starting new churches, and had also worked together on denominational issues, I saw Von on numerous occasions. Well before his death, Von had a number of physical problems that started the downhill slide. Many, many people prayed fervently for his health to improve. Still, Von slowly deteriorated and our concerns increased.

A year before he finally passed, Von confided in Michael that he knew he was dying. While he never conveyed exactly how he knew, Von seemed completely at peace with this awareness. Always interested in what was going on in the world, Von loved reading the newspaper and would often flip through the channels on television to get all the latest news. However, during the last several weeks of his life, Von quit reading the papers and watching the news altogether. Judy would lay the *Daily Oklahoman* by the recliner but Von wouldn't touch it. The TV was never turned on. Without fanfare, Von slipped into a quiet mode of expectation, waiting for the end. Finally, Mike decided that he should ask his father what was going on.

Von thoughtfully considered the inquiry and then explained that as he got closer to death, something within him was changing and he was becoming more of an inward person than an outward individual. The world of current events no longer held any interest for him. He couldn't exactly explain what was happening but he believed that the Holy Spirit was preparing him for eternal life. The outside world no longer mattered as he felt himself turning inward.

When Mike related this story to me, I was reminded of the many people I have observed who went through a similar process when their deaths took a greater amount of time. The phenomenon isn't unique to Von. I have even seen the dying at times not talk to their grandchildren because they were so internalized. In chapter 2, I described the story of my dear friend Nathalee as she prepared for death. When I saw her in the hospital during the last week of her life, Nat would open one eye and look at me as if I was interrupting something important going on inside her. She didn't want to be bothered; her focus was on another world. Von's experience paralleled this shift in orientation.

Von talked about his inner drift as being like a change in the seasons when winter gives way to spring. The individual knows that his time on Earth is coming to a close in this world and he or she becomes quite self-examining, looking at all the various facets of his or her life. Von described it as being a time of releasing everyone that he cared about into the Lord's care while he spent a considerable amount of time praying.

One afternoon late in Von's illness, Mike came over to visit him as he sat in his recliner. Beyond the recliner was a sliding double glass door that opened into the back yard. Von explained to his son that his world had drastically changed and become like the difference between being in the house and standing outdoors looking in. While Von was still in this physical world, he could see the spiritual world "out there" and with increasing clarity. Heaven was no longer something that he simply believed in; it had become a strong reality in his life. As his physical body shut down, that "other" realm grew in strength. Von described how he could already feel the closeness of relatives like his father and mother or older brother looking in through the glass. It was almost like he could see this world fading before the one that he was about to enter. While he didn't see these deceased dear relatives with his physical eyes, he sensed their nearness like people standing on the other side of the glass door.

Being in contact with those who had gone on before had come to have a profound meaning for Von Owen. Beginning his Christian life as an evangelical, he had followed the work of his son when Mike moved into a dimension of the Church that strongly emphasized the sacraments. The heart of our Sunday worship services is Holy Communion, where congregants come forward to kneel and receive the bread and wine from the chalice held by the hand of the pastor.

The transition from an evangelistic setting to a more liturgical service would stretch some people. Not Von. He loved every minute of this kind of worship. However, one Sunday Von found Holy Communion to be a particularly powerful spiritual experience and was deeply moved during the consecration of the elements by the words "Therefore we praise you, joining our voices with angels and archangels and all the company of heaven . . ." During the recitation of the Nicene Creed in every worship service, he affirmed that he believed in "the communion of the saints," an ongoing relationship that believers have with those who have preceded them in death. While these words of faith are often said in a rote manner, Von discovered that they promised an encounter in heaven with the multitudes of saints who died in other centuries. With time, Von developed a strong desire to meet and know these saints after he died.

As his death approached, Von's eagerness grew to reach through that partition that had become like the glass door in his bedroom. The pane of glass seemed to become steadily thinner until it was like the departed were lined up on the other side of the door waiting for him to step through. He had completely entered into a new sense of another reality and, even while he was alive on this earth, he knew that heaven waited at his fingertips.

While Von grew quieter and seemed less interested in the things of this world, he was changing in a deep way that impacted him to the core of his being. A disinterested relative might not have seen how drastically Von was actually changing. But by noting the details, asking questions and *changing his perspective* of the picture he was seeing, Von's son Mike learned from the experience and was able to recognize his father's deep changes. Again, perception changes what we see in the picture.

One of the last things that Von said during the final hours before he died was, "I will see you soon, Mom."

The Larger Picture

With Von's situation, we can read deeper into the picture and see that as his physical vitality decreased, his realization of eternity increased. He came to have an enduring sense that heaven was just beyond his fingertips. I'm not talking about an increase in what he believed, but an increase in absolute confidence in what he *knew* was there. While many people don't possess such an immediate awareness, one of the common elements in the near-death experiences of many people is that they see, feel or somehow experience this other dimension.

The story of Ron Wooten Green gives us another concrete example from which we can read and gather some important insights. Green served as a university professor and a Roman Catholic lay minister, and worked with the dying as a hospice chaplain. His excellent book *When the Dying Speak* begins with the story of his 51-year-old wife Dawn's struggle not long before her death. She had been waking up and talking to someone that Ron couldn't see. One night she was agitated and upset because she didn't know how to get from her bedroom to heaven when she died. The next day, Ron came home at noon and found Dawn sitting up in bed with a smile across her face. Ron assumed she must have received a call from one of their children.

"Oh, Ron. Those people who have been hanging around here have given me a ticket for the bus and invited me to go with them!"[1]

Ron writes that he didn't need to ask her where they were going. He had a clear enough perception of the situation to know that the bus was marked *Heaven Bound*.

Like Von Owen, Dawn Green's perception of the other side had become clear and striking. Her encounter had clarified a problem and set her free to come to the end of her life without worry or consternation. Dying had not slowed her down a notch. She'd seen the route to heaven before she crossed the line.

Let's look at another picture and then we'll review them in more detail.

Another dear friend is our financial planner Adrien Grout, Jr., a man who helped Margueritte and me prepare for retirement. Adrian is not only an expert in money matters but also at one time served in our church's ministry. Adrian is a man I deeply trust and whose advice I pay attention to. His father, Adrian Grout, Sr., had been the pastor at the same Wesleyan Methodist Church for 50 years, producing a large and successful church. When he became the pastor, he succeeded O. L. Ruth, who had been the pastor of the congregation for 32 years, leaving behind a church in excellent condition before he passed away. The two men had made a permanent mark on their community.

As Adrian Grout, Sr.'s life began to wind down, he became more and more feeble. Finally, as death approached, the only person present was his wife, Mable. With his eyes closed, Adrian's facial features took on the characteristics of one about to depart. Suddenly, he opened his eyes and sat up in bed. His face instantly became radiant.

"O. L!" Adrian greeted his old friend. "O. L. Ruth! How good to see you!"

Adrian looked to the side and began talking to his parents, Paul and Imma Grout, who had both been ministers before they died. "Why, Mom and Dad!" Adrian said with excitement. "You're here. How wonderful."

Mable saw nothing but knew her husband's vision was locked on eternity. She was certain that reality was unfolding before her eyes.

Adrian paused, held up his arms, and then suddenly exclaimed, "Blessed Jesus!" At that moment he fell back on the bed and was gone.

What happened? Adrian Grout, Sr., had reached across the line into heaven before he actually got there.

Shifting Perception

At the start of this chapter, our admonition was that *perception* changes what we see in a picture. Important clues can be easily overlooked the first time we look at the picture. Moreover, what's often most important seems so simple and obvious once it is identified, but prior to clarification, the significance of specific details may slip past. Let's take a second look at those pictures offered by Von, Dawn and Adrian, as well as the others we've read so far. What can we find that they all have in common? When reading the pictures in our photo album so far, what details present us with truths to be learned?

First, these accounts of heaven are concrete, not abstract. Views of heaven vary from a blissful Nirvana to the ancient idea of a vast protoplasmic substance floating out in space. Some suggest that we return to a kind of "oneness," like a drop of water returning to the ocean. None of the pictures we examined fits these more abstract descriptions.

It's notable that many of the snapshots we have read about in this book are far more like this world, containing some form, structure and shape. Often there are recognizable features that are solid and substantial.

Second, the pictures immediately demonstrate in fairly consistent ways that there's another world on the other side.

While its context changes from a physical environment to one that is spiritual, it is a realm in which the shape of human existence continues. The nature of how this happens certainly defies human imagination, but still it makes sense to us; it feels right to us because heaven is analogous to our world. We don't understand some of the differences and various dimensions of heaven but the evidence in the pictures fits our experiences developed in this world.

Also, these afterlife insights from the dying and returned tell us that "going to heaven" is as simple as stepping over a threshold, taking a bus trip or opening a door. The dying reach out to embrace people they once knew, or they get a ticket for the bus and then they are gone. Again, we can listen to these stories and make sense of them because what happens appears to fit into our experience of this world.

It's interesting to note that people who count themselves agnostics or atheists often change their minds after a near-death encounter. They have seen the other side and know that their previous doubts or rejection of the afterlife and God no longer fits the facts of their experiences. Having stepped into the beyond, these problematic questioners have seen a world that makes their free thinking irrelevant. Why? Because their time in this world now makes their encounters with eternity make sense.

Third, we see in consistent ways that heaven is filled with people. This was true of Von's, Dawn's and Adrian's encounters, as they were greeted by old friends, loved ones and, in Adrian's case, even the Lord Jesus Christ Himself. As far as we can tell, each person saw the faces of people they cared about.

In Von's case, he was even looking forward to meeting saints from centuries past.

This dimension tells us that relationships are important and that they continue. The Nicene Creed's affirmation that we believe in the "communion of the saints" affirms that the love once shared in this world will continue on into the next. How we have dealt with people, sought forgiveness, tried to restore broken relationships and been helpful to others has consequences for eternity. Heaven tells us, as does Scripture, that we must take the well-being of people very seriously.

Conclusion

During my undergraduate days, the college I attended had a peculiar view promoted through their philosophy courses. The professors taught that faith is based on convictions, not the facts. They rejected any physical evidence for faith as suspect. One professor taught that "no one can know." The idea that the resurrection of Jesus Christ was physical was rejected because the belief was too tangible. Faith must be held as a conjecture, or a pure belief, and facts were disallowed.

My experiences with the dying and those returned from near-death experiences challenge that idea. These snapshots offer anecdotal evidence of another variety. While faith is a matter of conviction, these encounters present data from the other side that is concrete and substantial. As the book of Hebrews 12:1 tells us, "we are surrounded by so great a cloud of witnesses" that bear witness to a reality greater than any human could imagine.

So far, we have observed four facts from studying the data and *reading the pictures*:

1. Our existence doesn't end; it only changes.
2. Heaven exists.
3. Heaven is concrete; it is not an abstraction.
4. Heaven is filled with people.

I believe the snapshots tell us we can trust these facts.

Note

1. Ron Wooten Green, *When the Dying Speak* (Chicago, IL: Loyola Press, 2001), p. 2.

CHAPTER TWELVE

The Seven Final Steps

With a disposition for assisting the departing, Patricia Ackerson, R.N., has been there when many, many people crossed over the line. For 40 years, she nursed the seriously ill and spent most of her time working with the dying. Growing up an Episcopalian, Patricia married a pastor now with the Communion of Evangelical Episcopal Churches and is a decidedly spiritual individual. Her wide-ranging career has taken her up and down the Eastern seaboard where she worked with many types of individuals as well as shared her Christian faith.

While employed with the Veterans Administration in Washington, D.C., Patricia Ackerson worked in the Department for Infectious Diseases, doing research on difficult illnesses. All her patients were infected with HIV and eventually died of AIDS. The work was demanding and would have emotionally strained anyone. Nevertheless, Patricia kept making her rounds, helping the dying during the final hours of their lives.

One afternoon, Patricia walked into the room of Andre, a dying man who called himself a black Muslim. She quickly ascertained that his time was short and he might not endure much longer than an hour. Lying on the hospital bed, Andre appeared to be running, even though he hadn't walked in months. AIDS patients often develop sarcoma cancers, in which one will develop cancers in supportive tissues such as cartilage, fat or muscle. Andre had some of these external tumors that had backed up his blood, creating an enlarged leg condition something like elephantitis.

Patricia sat down and watched Andre for a minute before asking him, "Where are you going?"

"I've got to catch the bus," Andre said. His pace picked up and then Andre stopped and started dozing.

Andre's birth name was Keith. Like so many of his friends, he called himself a Muslim although the label actually had little to do with religious beliefs and had more to do with his cultural identification as an African American. This was true of Keith, or Andre as he now called himself.

By the time Andre awoke from his nap, Patricia had checked many of his vital signs and knew his life was almost finished. She leaned over and asked, "Do you know about the Lord Jesus Christ? Do you know him as your Savior?"

"Oh, yes, ma'am," Andre said. "I do." He dropped off to sleep again.

When he awoke, Andre started flapping his arms like he was flying. "Got to see Jesus," he whispered to Patricia.

The nurse leaned over the bed and said, "Andre, you can go anytime you want."

The young man looked up, smiled, and didn't take two more breaths. He closed his eyes and was gone.

Andre may have identified himself by another designation, but when it came to "crossing the river," it appeared as though he believed Jesus Christ was the path over. These final moments can take many forms, but in this case, Patricia observed peace, joy and relief. She had a sense that something extremely important was happening with these patients like Andre as she watched them peacefully depart this life.

The Seven Final Steps

Patricia Ackerson's experiences, such as the story of Andre, are like Cindi Pursely's, as well as many others. And again, that's what catches my attention: *The similarities are striking.* As I explored these commonalities for myself, I found that they reflect Scripture and can be considered biblically accurate.

Up to this point in our study of these pictures, the photo album has implied or directly established four facts:

1. There is another realm waiting for believers. Heaven exists.
2. Individuals are transformed. Our existence doesn't end; it only changes.
3. Heaven is analogous to Earth and is concrete, not abstract.
4. People we've known are there; and heaven is filled with people.

In addition, the parallels in these dying people's experiences, in the stories I've witnessed personally, in the stories of the people I've interviewed, and in the published research of so many doctors and professors that we've reviewed, outline for us seven final steps or functions that we will likely face on the other side.

Chapter Twelve

1. People Will Meet a Loved One from Their Past or Someone Who Loves Them

In the encounters I've observed, near-death survivors report meeting a deceased person known earlier in their lives. Like Don Piper's finding his grandfather and a high school friend killed in a car wreck, we can anticipate a loved one waiting with his hands out to welcome us. If the person wasn't a part of one of our personal relationships, he or she is still waiting for us with love. However, we may not always have directly known this person in a way that we can recall.

During open-heart surgery, Lynn succumbed to death and discovered that a man calling himself her uncle was waiting on the other side. She had no idea such an uncle had existed in her family. Lynn was surprised to find him in a military uniform accompanied by another companion. This unknown relative and his friend offered her encouragement. The uncle told Lynn that the child with him was his. He related that everything was okay with them. When Lynn woke up alive, she remembered all of these details and was surprised because she'd never heard of either of these people. She talked to her family afterward to learn more.

When Lynn asked her family about the man, there was a stunned silence. The uncle had been killed during World War II and her family had kept his existence a secret. No records remained of the fact that he had been married to her aunt, who had had a miscarriage. Even speaking the uncle's name had been forbidden. The family felt total shock upon hearing Lynn's accurate and detailed description of the man they had attempted to eradicate as ever having existed. The aunt's husband (who had always claimed to be her only husband) never spoke to Lynn again. Nevertheless, Lynn had met someone from her past who greeted her even though she had not known the man existed.[1]

2. The Dying Do Not Meet Someone Who Is Still Alive

No one *ever* mentions encountering a living person. The person met on the other side has always died. In all the incidences I have observed, or in my conversations with the professionals who attended the dying, this has always been true. People who have researched these phenomena find this to be universally the case.

In absolute contrast to the horror movies that pop up around Halloween, these experiences of transition are not weird, wild or spooky. There's no background music with strange noises or bizarre strobe lights flashing. Everyone witnessing these final moments in the cycle of life encounters a normal process that is not frightening.

The fact that this pattern is predictable takes these experiences out of the realm of the delusional. Hallucinations take on a wide range of possibilities, but generally the observer thinks he or she is seeing a living person who actually isn't there. This difference adds meaning to these near-death encounters.

3. The Dying Come to Understand Why the Already-Deceased Have Appeared with Them

As the dying enter an out-of-body existence, their movements might better be described as "floating." They move like clouds, whether they find themselves sliding down a tunnel or appearing before heaven's gates. As if propelled by thought rather than muscular movement, they encounter a deceased person or persons and communicate with these individuals who went on before them. Don Piper not only met his grandfather and high school friend Mike Wood, but he also found his Native American grandmother who had been released from being stooped over because of osteoporosis and had been freed of her old-age wrinkles. The presence of these loved ones imparted a message. As a pastor, Don had led many funerals where he said the words "To be absent from the body is to be present with the Lord to those who love and know him." The radiance in their faces communicated with him and imparted new meaning to these final words said during a funeral. The experience stayed with him even after he returned to this world.

One of the common events with those who spent a significant amount of time in eternity is that they reached a point where they were told they had a choice whether to stay or come back. Usually, they had a clear sense of a mission yet to be accomplished. In the Barbara Walters ABC special *Where Is Heaven?*, Walters related the story of Elizabeth Taylor's near-death experience. After departing from this world, Ms. Taylor wanted to stay but was sent back to complete something that she hadn't done. Shortly after her return, Ms. Taylor began a fervent campaign to raise funds to fight AIDS. Because of her journey beyond, Elizabeth Taylor says she has no fear of dying today. This kind of renewed purpose is common as the deceased person met on the other side often communicates a purpose for the person's return to Earth.

4. Returning Persons Cannot Give a Good Physical Description of the Deceased They Encountered, Though They Clearly Knew Them

Heavenly experiences with the departed seem to be an encounter with the *essence* of the person. The observer has an out-of-body experience. Because our everyday world is filled with commercials about eyeliners, make-up, the latest fashions, the latest style in shoes, etc., we tend to be stuck on external appearance. The secular world is a highly superficial realm that seldom pauses to wonder if it's possible that there's more to people that we can see.

What might be the essence of a person? Let me give you an example of how I've experienced that question. When I was 25, I could look in a mirror and see a person I knew well: dark, thick beard; tan skin; black hair. I would have known that face anywhere. It was me. Then I got to be 45 and looked in the mirror again, but there was something wrong with the mirror. The face wasn't reflecting back correctly: My black beard was turning gray; the texture of my hair was changing; my cheeks were dropping. Then at 65 everything went wrong! I now have a white beard and gray hair. My entire face has gone south! What happened? The face I see now and the essence of Robert Wise (preserved in my mind) are different. The truth is that my memory stores that essence no matter how my appearance is altered by time.

Time may improve or dissipate our essence, but our essence stays with us. We all know who we are, even though our appearances may change radically! The dying appear to encounter this unchanging reality when they meet others during their afterlife journey. When they return and describe what they've seen, it often sounds more like a dream. I believe this is an important clue that shortly we will consider more fully.

5. The Dying Must Deal with Their Past or They Will Have a Difficult Time Dying

As many people approach death, they close their eyes and drift into their own inner world. Often, they don't want relatives or friends to bring them back from the important work they are doing. Sometimes they will tell us they are watching "movies" of their life being played in their minds. Even though they appear to be asleep, they are hard at work cleaning the skeletons out of their closets and getting their lives in order before it's all over.

In chapter 3, we shared the final moments in Victor Parks's life. The family thought that he was unconscious but the visiting nurse noticed that his eyelashes kept fluttering. Victor reported to her that he was watching movies of his life being rerun in his head and didn't want the family to interrupt him. He could slow the review process down when the contents got a little ragged and issues had to be worked out. Before he died, Victor Parks reevaluated his entire life and this made his passing much easier.

People tend to die the way they lived. If a person has been judgmental, condemnation may surface. Where a person may have harbored unconfessed areas of transgression, the hidden problems will push to the surface. Everyone needs to clean the rubbish out of their closets today because it will come tumbling out of the closet at the end of their lives in a more painful way. Dealing with the need immediately certainly beats trying to sort it out at death's door.

One of the most helpful things that hospice and hospital chaplains do is to encourage these confrontations with the unspoken secret details of our lives. Rev. Ray Wade, a chaplain with Preferred Hospice in Oklahoma City, was assigned a dying man who had been abused and had a difficult family experience. The referral sheet suggested that he might want to avoid the man until it became necessary, as the patient could become quite aggressive. Ray soon discovered that the fellow had been a cheat in business and had been married a number of times. Also, it became apparent that an abusive father had never expressed love for this man and that the rejection had cut him deeply.

When Ray walked into his room, a piece of watermelon was sitting on a table next to the bed. Ray glanced at the plate.

"That's mine!" the man barked.

"I used to raise watermelon," Ray said.

"I did too," the man said in surprise.

"My favorite was Charleston Gray," Ray answered.

"Mine too," the astonished patient replied.

After this exchange, Ray was able to cut through the ice and begin a meaningful conversation. Their relationship deepened. One afternoon, Ray asked his charge what he missed most.

"My wife," the man mumbled and broke into tears.

From there on the conversations became personal and the hard patient softened and later prayed with the chaplain to accept Jesus. Ray called this moment his "watermelon conversion." A change in perspective made all the difference in how this man saw his life and, consequently, how he died.

6. As People Start to Die, They Withdraw from This World

In chapter 11, we observed the story of Von Owen's death. His last year was a time of withdrawal from the world, and this example is instructive. Over the 40 years of my public ministry, I have probably observed this tendency as much as any other. In the case of my friend Nathalee, the final weeks of her life were a turning away from this world until she was finally gone. Often, we may interpret this pulling away as the onslaught of a growing illness or as the body shutting down (and certainly this happens), but the dynamic in the person's mind finds the person distancing himself or herself from the world around him or her.

Von Owen's gradual awareness of the departed saints waiting as if people were waving from the other side of the sliding glass door is particularly insightful. During his life, Von was a practical person who was not given to mystical experiences. A pragmatic evangelical, his approach to the Christian faith was straightforward and orthodox. Consequently, Von was not a candidate for having an unusual experience at the end of his life. Nevertheless, the long period of withdrawing from the physical world prepared him for enlarged spiritual insight.

It is also interesting to note that after near-death experiences, people who returned came back with a dramatically changed perception of what was important. No longer fearing death, they became more sensitive and others-centered people who reached out in ways that they had never done before. A personal encounter with death appears universally to open eyes to a greater purpose that has been missed or not understood.

Withdrawing from the world at the end of life appears to help the dying accomplish this purpose.

We don't need to worry or fear when someone we love starts turning away from us as he or she is dying. This is normal, and it appears to be healthy, as the dying person prepares for death.

7. Near-Death Experiences Transform Doubts

As we mentioned earlier, atheists and agnostics change their minds about the afterlife after such an experience, almost universally. Others come back with drastically altered perceptions, feelings and responses, as well. Some people get angry or depressed that they have returned. Occasionally, folks don't feel they can talk about their experiences and may suppress them for a period of time. Others are thrilled that they had such a remarkable experience and may be in awe of what has occurred. Many are humbled by the extraordinary events, while others become evangelistic about their discoveries.

Faith comes from a decision that we make for ourselves. It remains a private area in our free will. However, these near-death encounters suggest that the journey into heaven erases that dark residue of life in the physical world. Therefore, I conclude that the transformation of doubt into conviction is part of our final steps.

Dee Dee's Story

While not a story of doubt, the essence of the Seven Steps is contained in the following account. Not all the steps are here, but there are enough for us to develop another specific image in our minds of what may be ahead.

In the summer of 1981, Dee Dee Bailey suffered a second kidney attack that put her in the hospital, and upon arriving at the hospital it turned out that she was also suffering from kidney stones, doubling her concern.

Mary D. Bailey had always gone by the name Dee Dee. She joined our Servants in Prayer healing group at the church, absorbing instruction in how to minister to the sick, and became an ardent intercessor for the ill.

Her physician was leaving town but told Dee Dee that another doctor would insert a catheter to help her with her problem. Unfortunately, the standby doctor forgot and the catheter was never placed. Dee Dee's temperature shot up to 107 degrees and she went into convulsions. Toxic shock syndrome set in and septicaemia raced through her system. Dee Dee went quickly from a painful but treatable illness to a desperately fatal condition.

At 7:30 on this particular Sunday morning, her doctor rushed in to begin a procedure to regulate her heart, but blood poison had already been released into her system. Dee Dee's kidneys shut down and her blood pressure started dropping. Her body was dying.

Her mother, Donna, called the church and reported how serious the problem had become. During the worship time, it was announced that Dee Dee was in trouble, and the entire congregation started praying for her, right in the middle of the service. Back at the hospital, Dee Dee's blood pressure fell through the bottom.

Dee Dee Bailey died.

And then it was as if Dee Dee sat up in bed, even though she saw her body lying flat on the mattress of the hospital bed. She saw tears forming in the eyes of the nurse.

"We're losing her, aren't we?" the nurse asked.

The doctor didn't answer but kept working furiously, calling out to her and calling her Mary, even though she didn't normally go by that name. At that moment Dee Dee started leaving this world.

Two large angels appeared and escorted her from the hospital room. Gently but firmly, they led her into a tunnel of light. As Dee Dee floated along, she heard music, but the sound was a thousand times more magnificent than anything she'd heard before. The music overwhelmed her with an awesome sense of thanksgiving. While she had never heard the language before, she could understand exactly what was being sung. She reported that the experience felt wonderful and that all the pain from the kidney stones was gone.

At the other end of the tunnel, she stepped out. In front of her stood Jesus Christ with His arms open and extended toward her. Dee Dee raced to Him and they hugged. Somehow without words Jesus communicated how much He loved her.

"It isn't your time," Jesus finally said.

Dee Dee didn't want to leave and realized that she could stay right there forever.

"It isn't your time," He repeated. "I need you to return and feed my sheep."

Dee Dee looked up at Jesus and into the most beautiful eyes she had ever seen. Then she felt the sensation of being slammed back into her body, and her own eyes popped open.

"Oh my God!" the nurse exclaimed. "Her eyes are open."

The doctor had just stuck a needle into Dee Dee's chest, shooting adrenaline directly into her heart. Immediately, Dee Dee was rushed to the ICU, where she began her recovery. However, even in those moments the eyes of Christ stayed fresh in her mind.

Today, Dee Dee paints and one of her next tasks is to paint a portrait of the eyes of Christ. But most of Dee Dee's time is absorbed with "feeding the sheep." She has a life assignment to help people meet Jesus Christ and she pursues this work with college students at the University of Oklahoma. And because she is also a survivor of breast cancer, Dee Dee works with women who have been diagnosed with cancer. In all these works, her after-life experience continues to communicate the life of Christ to people even to this day.

Conclusion

For many readers, this list of seven steps will not sound like taking steps at all. Rather, each experience should be seen as a wonderful invitation to fulfillment. Certainly they are that! I find myself amazed that people all over the world of vastly different backgrounds report these same events and that they can be compiled into a straightforward list. These steps certainly offer us pictures that are awesome to behold.

I find it worthwhile to review these seven steps and ask myself if I am ready for such experiences. Have I done what I must to prepare myself for the final times of my life? Because death may come at an unexpected time, I know that I need to do so.

Probably the hardest step to deal with of the seven steps I outlined is confronting our past and making sure all things are in order. But as difficult as it might sound, anyone can do this if he or she has the courage to do so. Looking into yesterday doesn't mean attempting to change what was there or being sorry about what we couldn't help. But there are always times when we've been the victim as well as the victimizer. Sometimes, we can't go back to those experiences because the people we were involved with won't allow us to do so. However, we can make sure that our heart and intentions are in the right place. Doing so is part of what Jesus taught us when He said, "he who does the truth comes to the light, that his deeds may be clearly seen, that they have been done in God" (John 3:21). This exercise is part of walking in the light.

Note
1. P. M. H. Atwater, *The Complete Idiot's Guide to Near-Death Experiences* (New York: Alpha Books, 2000), pp. 244-245.

The Greatest Story

In the previous pages I've shared a number of astonishing stories, but have you heard the greatest after-death story ever told?

This is the story about a man who had been falsely charged with a crime he didn't commit, but it didn't keep the authorities from proceeding with his execution. Authorities rushed the trial and botched the sentencing as well. Even the man's friends ran in fear because the police were everywhere and in no mood to tolerate dissent. These were faithful friends who had pledged to-the-death loyalty and then simply disappeared. The court officers moved in quickly to fulfill the death sentence, but the process of execution proved to be drawn out and the man's death was excruciating. Once the man had been pronounced dead, his body was hauled to a nearby mortuary. The morticians didn't have much time to prepare the body in the way that local customs demanded. Consequently, they stuck the body in another person's mausoleum. As far as the police were concerned, that was the end of the matter, although they posted guards to make sure no funny business happened over the weekend.

Three days later some friends returned to add a few flowers to their friend's new grave. To their shock, the door had been torn off the grave! They stuck their heads inside and found the shroud piled up to one side. The body was gone! Two strange-looking fellows sat inside and told them not to be afraid. They knew who the women were looking for, but they said that the man was no longer dead. They said he had come back to life! These women immediately ran through town shouting the amazing story about what had happened to their friend!

Well, you see where this story is going and you've figured out that it's the RSV (Robert's Standard Version) in contemporary form describing the condensed accounts Matthew, Mark, Luke and John tell about the resurrection of Jesus Christ from the dead. Of all the stories we've reviewed so far, this is the standard by which we measure the truth. The Christian faith is centered in the conviction that Jesus of Nazareth was betrayed, falsely accused, crucified under Pontius Pilate, buried, and on the third day rose from the dead. The Gospel of John starts in the *Phillips* translation by saying, "At the beginning God expressed himself. That personal expression, that word, was with God, and was God, and he existed with God from the beginning . . . in him appeared life, and this life was the light of mankind. The light still shines in the darkness and the darkness has never put it out" (John 1:1-2,4-5).

The Ultimate Measuring Stick

Christians believe that the light of Christ illumines all darkness and they measure the unknown by what is revealed in this light. Therefore, we must test these experiences we've being considering by this standard of truth. We measure the validity of such stories by how they match what happened in the Bible, and specifically, because of our topic, by what happened in Jesus' life and resurrection.

The resurrection is so central to Christian faith that it appears in 17 of the New Testament books and is implicit in most of the remaining books. The initial witness of the four Gospels tells the same story from different points of view. With the exception of 2 Thessalonians, Titus and Philemon, all the writings of Paul refer to the resurrection. In Paul's epistles, he never even attempts to prove the resurrection, as the entire Christian community already accepted it as the bedrock of their convictions. All the major creeds of the Christian Church include the resurrection as the central fact of their faith.

While we have already raised questions about the experiences of the dying being the result of drugs or hallucinations, the resurrection of Jesus of Nazareth takes this inquiry to a higher level. For 2,000 years, the Christian community has proclaimed that the resurrection of Jesus was a fact that happened in history. At the same time, the resurrection has also been described as supra-historic, meaning that it also transcends time. In his book *Church Dogmatics,* Karl Barth described the resurrection as "fulfilled time" breaking into everyday life.[1] The idea is that Jesus had a foot in both worlds: Earth and heaven. After He died, Jesus returned in a transformed manner from a realm where there are no clocks. Subsequently, while we can talk about what happened in normal language, the event actually exceeds all forms of verbal expression.

Does this sound somewhat familiar? In the near-death experiences we've been talking about, each person crossed a line after which it is difficult for language to fully express what occurred on the other side. Everyday speech won't cover exactly what they saw.

A Blueprint for Eternity

Taking the contents of the New Testament, many Christians have attempted to develop a blueprint for how the final moments of individual lives fit into the end of the world and the final great resurrection at the end of history. These viewpoints have differed so widely that entire denominations have been produced because their ideas are unique from another group's.

For example, some groups expect us to die and be "asleep" until the very end of time, until Jesus returns. Other groups are convinced that at the moment of death we enter heaven. I find it significant that in all of the near-death experiences and stories, the individual immediately entered the other side and there was no discontinuity in their awareness and experience of events; but it must be noted that some did need help from another to "cross over."

The Rev. Lawrence Anthony Wheeler was a minister, teacher, and missionary with the Seventh-day Adventist denomination for his entire career. Born on Christmas Eve in 1909, he retained a giant personality throughout his entire life. As was true of his group of believers, Wheeler expected eventually to die, be buried and sleep until the great resurrection at the end of time. Along the way, he and his wife had two children. Where he had been a physically and emotionally strong person, Wheeler's last years became a struggle because of strokes that left him in a deteriorated condition. Eventually, Wheeler had to be cared for in a private facility in Roseburg, Oregon, where he developed a chronic infection and needed to be isolated. Finally, his strength diminished until he had to be fed by the nurse because it was impossible for him to lift his arms.

His daughter Marjorie Wheeler Raymond told me his final story. When she received the call from the nursing home, Marjorie knew she didn't have much time left with her father. However, as soon as she started for Roseburg, it began snowing fiercely. The snow forced her to pull into a roadside restaurant to consider what to do next. While drinking a cup of coffee, she silently prayed, "Lord, if You want me to make it to Roseburg, You've got to make it stop." When she came out of the café, the snow had stopped. Marjorie decided it was a sign to keep going.

When she reached the nursing home, the staff knew the seriousness of the situation and told her that her father was only "waiting for her." Marjorie knew the signs of death and instantly recognized that her father didn't have long to live. His feet were already cooling. She asked that a sign be placed on the door and that the two of them be left alone.

After a few moments, her father began looking at the ceiling as if he were looking up into the sky. An unexpected expression of joy suddenly flooded his face. Even though his strength was completely gone, Lawrence Wheeler began raising his arms. A new capacity infused his body. He raised both arms and then lowered them slowly, only to raise them again with a smile on his face. For an entire hour, Wheeler was in communication with what only he could see. At the end, there was no death rattle or sign of dying. Lawrence Wheeler was taken home quickly and peacefully.

In contrast to what both Marjorie and her father expected, it appeared as if Wheeler went straight to heaven, though we don't know for sure. My point is not to demonstrate that one theological perspective is better than another; I am simply looking at the evidence and attempting to understand what it says. Certainly Lawrence Wheeler's final experience, as Marjorie perceived it, fits the outline of Scripture. The Gospel of Luke reports that, as Jesus was being crucified, He said to the thief, "Assuredly, I say to you, today you will be with Me in Paradise" (Luke 23:43). Three days later Jesus returned. The picture of an immediate transition to the other side clearly fits the Bible's picture of eternity.

A Transformed Existence

Whether the dying person is an adult or a child, another common denominator of this experience is that the dying find themselves in an out-of-body type of existence. People in this state report feeling as if they're floating along with the ease of a cloud. Sometimes, they will suddenly find themselves at the top of the room looking down on what is happening below or they may be listening to conversations outside in the hallway that they later verify happened. Often, they will be looking down on their own bodies that they know are dead. Our question here is, Does this fit with what Scripture says about death and eternity? First, let's review another brief story about someone who experienced this phenomenon.

At around the age of eight or nine, Carl Allen Pierson of Hinton, West Virginia, was struck by lightning. Running through a thunderstorm with a metal washtub over his head, Carl felt the full impact of a thunderbolt knocking him through the air. The next thing Carl knew, he was hovering above his family, who had gathered over his fallen body. After they took Carl's body to a doctor's office, he continued to watch, floating above his own body until he was resuscitated.[2] Such occurrences are common in near-death experiences, and they seem to point toward a transformation of the individual's existence after death, as one goes from the physical body to a spiritual one.

The Gospels give us some insight into the nature of Jesus' resurrected body. While the four accounts do not give us what we would today consider to be scientific evidence, they obviously show that something more dramatic happened than just the resuscitation of a corpse. Reanimation, which is the same as resuscitation, does mean bringing a person back to life. However, resurrection is far more significant. It is the reunion of body and spirit certainly, but the spirit is reunited with a *different* body. Jesus' resurrected body could still be traced back to who He was before death from the scars of crucifixion on His hands and feet, but still, His body had been transformed. One of the mysterious paradoxes of the Christian faith is that the resurrection of Jesus seemed to produce both the *same and a different* body.

When you carefully read the Gospel accounts, you pick up amazing differences in how Jesus' resurrection body appeared to function from what it did before death. John's Gospel tells us that Mary Magdalene stood outside the tomb weeping when she found it empty. When Jesus appeared, she thought Him to be the gardener. Not until Jesus spoke her name did Mary recognize Him. Obviously, He was *both alike and different in appearance* from what He had been before. That night, the apostles (except Thomas who wasn't with the group) locked every door in the house to keep anyone from breaking in and catching them, because they were terrified. Suddenly, Jesus stood among them. Eight days later, Jesus appeared to Thomas, who refused to believe it was Him until he saw the wounds in His hands. In a similar vein, the Emmaus Road event tells us the story of two disciples discussing the crucifixion on the afternoon of Easter day. They did not recognize Jesus as He appeared and explained all that had occurred. Only later, when He was breaking bread with them did the two men know who He was. Then, immediately Jesus disappeared.

What can we make of this? Theologians and preachers have explored the meaning of the resurrection from many angles over the centuries. However, for our purposes in this book, we can note that what has been called an out-of-body experience is amazingly similar to the resurrected body of Jesus. For example, when Mary Magdalene encounters Him, Jesus tells her, "Do not cling to Me, for I have not yet ascended to My Father" (John 20:17). Obviously, something about His body was significantly different. As He was transformed after death, Jesus came back with the ability to walk back and forth between the world of the living and the curtain of death. He could abruptly appear and then instantly vanish. While some recognized Him, some didn't. Also, the end of Matthew's Gospel has a telltale sentence we would do well to notice. Well after Easter day, Jesus told the apostles that He would meet them in Galilee. When the group came to the meeting, Matthew tells us, "when they saw Him, they worshiped Him; but *some doubted*" (28:17, emphasis added).

And until the end of time, such will always be the case: some people will always doubt.

However, we must note that there is an important difference between what happened with Jesus and others who came back from near-death experiences in the Bible. For example, Lazarus had one of the most significant after-death experiences of anyone in the recorded past or present (see John 11:5-44). As amazing as was his return after three days in a tomb, there is a big difference: Jesus resuscitated Lazarus, while Jesus was resurrected. People such as Carl Allen Pierson return to go on being what they were until they come to their ultimate death. However, Paul writes in 1 Corinthians that the resurrection actually produces an incorruptible body. This is forever the difference between the resurrection of Jesus the Christ and the near-death experiences we have examined thus far.

Living in a Spiritual World

How do people born in the twentieth or twenty-first century make sense out of talk that sounds like it came out of a world of superstition before the Medieval Age? We live in the age of computers and rocket ships that take astronauts to the moon. People shoot down the highway twice as fast as anybody traveled in the 1920s. The life span of the American public has extended nearly two decades from two centuries ago. In our modern world, do you still believe in a spiritual realm? Can you follow all this near-death talk of a "transition" from one world to the next and not think you've dropped back into the age of the pharaohs and pyramids? I believe that there is an active spiritual world that is just beyond our reach, and I read these stories and experiences with an openness to the mystery of eternity, while always checking the facts against the Bible. I believe this is the lens through which we can best understand these near-death experiences and what they can teach us about death, life and eternity with God.

At some point in my life's journey, I came to the conviction that love is the greatest natural reality we encounter in this world. Can you slice it up, eat a cupful for breakfast or hang it on your wall? No, because love is intangible and abstract. Still, I believe that love is the ultimate source of meaning, so much so that it lead me to believe that there is a dimension of final truth that stands behind and beyond everything we see. I came to understand that if my perceptions were going to be accurate, I must readily anticipate that the spiritual world, the realm of angels, shadows, the unexpected and the unseen, will somehow have an effect on what is observable around me.

Consequently, I came to expect eternity not to be "somewhere out there" or "far up there" or in some far-off place in the universe. I believe it is close by, even in front of us, just beyond the tips of our fingers, yet unobservable. To put it another way, I believe that eternity is more like an unseen dimension. To be more precise, Earth is only a single aspect of the immeasurableness of God's world. We know that the third dimension is an experience of depth. We can mathematically calculate a fourth, fifth and sixth dimension (and many more) that we cannot experience with our eyes or sense of touch. Through my experiences and research, I find heaven to be more of that order. When people are starting to die, something remarkable begins to happen to their sense of perception. Folks like Lawrence Wheeler develop the ability "to see" beyond anything their eyes or convictions have previously seen. They develop a kind of discernment, a cognizance, an ability to penetrate beyond the boundaries of this world and reach into eternity.

This is a discipline and a shift in perception that we can begin to cultivate in our lives now. In fact, this is what Jesus Christ did throughout His life.

And Where Did Jesus Go?

Scripture affirms that Jesus Christ ascended to the right hand of God the Father Almighty and was given a name that is above every name so that every knee in both heaven and Earth should bow before Him (see Phil. 2:9-11). The period of His resurrection appearances proved to be of a great magnitude. Jesus was seen by all 12 apostles, by 500 others and by Saul whose name was changed to Paul after his encounter with the risen, exalted Christ. The book of Acts tells us that at His ascension, Jesus made a final appearance, and then before the eyes of His apostles and disciples, Jesus went into heaven (see Acts 1:9-11).

However, during the three-day period between Good Friday and Easter, the Scripture tells us something additional happened. The Bible relates that Jesus preached to those who had already died (see 1 Pet. 3:19; 4:6). The Scripture speaks of this as a descent in contrast to His later ascension into heaven. The Church affirms this reality in the Apostles Creed when believers say, "He suffered under Pontius Pilate, was crucified, dead and buried. He descended into hell [or to the dead]." The Scripture teaches us that Jesus went to the realm of dark and preached to the departed. Different theologians can argue about what Jesus preached, but the Bible affirms a realm of judgment that we've observed that some people have encountered. Once again, the near-death experience matches Scripture.

What Shall We Say?

Turning back to the first letter of John, the Bible tells us that "this is the testimony: that God has given us eternal life, and this life is in his Son. He who has the Son has life; he who has not the Son of God does not have life" (1 John 5:11-12). Obviously, Scripture wants believers to know that God gave them eternal life. Anyone who has come into a personal relationship with Jesus Christ has been given this gift. The apostle John's certainty about these final matters gives us another clue about the value of these snapshots of eternity. These pieces of data offer us assurance that we're not going to hell, rather we can be recipients of something mysterious and wonderful—we can live with God for eternity.

Notes
1. Karl Barth, *Church Dogmatics* (Edinburgh, UK: T & T Clark, 1956) vol. I, no. 2, p. 115.
2. P. M. H. Atwater, *Children of the New Millennium,* self-published, 1998, available from Dr. Atwater, P.O. Box 7691, Charlottesville, VA 22906-7691.

Pieces that Don't Fit

There are a few loose ends in how some of these near-death stories fit together. A few pieces that don't fit quite right.

Because that's the kind of world we live in. Volcanoes erupt and earthquakes rumble out of nowhere and people die. Every spring, tornadoes rip across America, killing people and destroying millions of dollars of property. Tsunamis sweep in and wipe out entire towns and regions. The bottom line is that we live in an unfinished and incomplete world that is constantly in a state of flux.

Stephen W. Hawking, holder of Newton's Chair as Professor of Mathematics at Cambridge ended his book *A Brief History of Time* by saying, "We find ourselves in a bewildering world." Nobel Prize winners from Simon van der Meer to Weinberg, with his unified theories of electromagnetic force, on to Albert Einstein, who died with no final explanation of the relationship between magnetism and the universe, will tell us our world is filled with contradictions, but that doesn't stop scientists from exploring truths. So when we see our world's best minds still grappling with unsolved issues, naturally we can expect to grapple with our own unsolved issues when it comes to talking about near-death experiences.

Could we expect less of such an unmeasurable and nebulous issue as crossing the line between life and death? At the same time, we want to try to erase as many of the question marks as possible.

A Piece that Doesn't Fit

Reverend Norman Neaves is a pastor, and has been at one particular church nearly his entire career. He founded the United Methodist Church of the Servant, which, over nearly 40 years, has grown into one of the denomination's largest congregations. During this time, he was pastor and friend to a man named Gary Dage. On Labor Day 1992, Dage was the chief administrative assistant for Congressman Glen English. Congressman English had gone to Western Oklahoma on a political foray when Dage sensed he was having a heart attack. Rushing to the hospital in Elk City, Dage struggled with incredible pain that would not stop. Later he described what followed as being like walking from one life into another. Nothing ended; he simply made a transition, because he never knew when he died.

As the pain stopped, a wonderful sense of peace came over him and Dage knew he was somewhere other than the hospital. While this unexpected realm was dark, there was nothing scary. Rather, it was extremely soothing. Dage was moving and yet he wasn't moving. Ahead of him, Dage could see an arch and beyond the entryway was the inviting glow of a gentle light. He wanted to cross the arch and enter this new world, but Dage began thinking about his family. He deeply loved his wife, Susan, and their three children, Deborah, Don and Diana. He didn't want to leave them.

As Dage came to this final point of departure, his family crossed before him, as if they were blocking the archway. Even his two-year-old grandson, Jake, stood with them. Dage knew they were blocking his way to keep him from going through. At that moment, he heard a voice calling, "Mr. Dage! Mr.Dage!" When he opened his eyes, a nurse was bending over him applying electro-shock to stimulate his heart. Dage was back in this world. Later, the nurse told him that his heart had stopped beating and he had been dead. When Dage related his story to Rev. Neaves, he called it a death experience.

After he was released from the hospital, Dage met with Neaves at an Oklahoma City restaurant to share his experience. While telling Neaves the story with all the details, Dage said that he would never fear death again. Neaves shared with me that following this near-death encounter, Dage made important and significant changes in his life. Susan Dage told me that she had no doubt that this amazing encounter had happened to her husband and knew that his unusual departure was genuine.

In November 2001, Gary Dage succumbed to lung cancer. He had smoked all of his life and at age 63, the illness eventually caught up with him. During the final months of his life, Neaves continued to be his pastor and visited with him again and again. Dage never exhibited dread or apprehension. Through the entire process, he remained happy, with a smile on his face. Near the end, Dage began talking with someone on the other side that only he could see. He talked to whoever was there in a happy, thoughtful way and then died peacefully.

In an earlier chapter, I observed that near-death travelers don't meet the living in heaven, and yet Dage appeared to meet his family after his own death. Still, I don't find that Gary's story violates this fact. I would interpret the appearance of his family members *before* he crossed the arch as being more like symbols in a dream. Was he dead? The nurse said he was. But his family was part of his sense of need to return to this world and so the nurse could bring him back. If this interpretation is correct, you can see how the dreamlike images and the afterlife experience merge and overlap.

A number of years ago, I spent time with a group of Benedictine Monks in Pecos, New Mexico. They had taken on the unusual task of attempting to coordinate psychoanalytic thought with the Christian faith, and they had come to believe that dreams were an important aspect of self-understanding. I lived with them for a time and participated in the life of their monastery as I studied how these disciplines might interrelate. Following this period, I studied dreams at the Jung Institute in Kusnacht, Switzerland, attempting to understand a dimension of personality and thinking that had eluded me earlier in my life. I found that while some dreams seem to lead us nowhere, a properly understood dream can be a powerful tool or way of thinking in the discipline of self-understanding and can lead to profound insights. This form of thinking, not uncommon to most of us, is called *intuition*.

In contrast to syllogistic logic, intuition is the inner ability to reach conclusions that arise out of the depths of our personality. Intuition is not unlike having a hunch that proves to be correct. Intuitive thoughts pop up in the mind. It's that strange sense of knowing that parents sometimes get when their children are doing something wrong. Intuitive people naturally seek meaning and purpose that gives form and direction to actions that are happening. Intuition is a powerful inner way "to know."

The language of the world of intuition is often symbolic, and symbols often seem to carry or embody many layers of meaning; probing these layers is what brings insight. Some people believe that the things we experience in our dreams are symbolic alarms trying to put us in touch with important areas of our lives that need our attention. Here's the key point as it concerns our discussion in this book: When a person is working through the meaning of a dream, I've found from my research that it can be similar to the experience of a near-death journey. Like in dreams, the images and locations and events from a near-death journey can be ripe with symbolic insight and meaning.

Another Piece: Communication Back from Eternity

Scripture forbids attempts at communicating with the deceased as we have already noted. Old Testament passages like Leviticus 20:27 or Deuteronomy 18:11 make this very clear. Necromancy is an attempt to learn from the dead information that could influence forthcoming events in this world. Trying to turn the dead into fortune-tellers is absolutely condemned in Scripture.

However, one of the loose ends is that rare moment when it seems as if the deceased are attempting to relate some message *to us*. As strange as it sounds, there are times when it appears such communication is happening. These are not spooky horror stories from Edgar Allen Poe but the experiences of normal people who stumble across something unexplainable. Let me share a couple of examples.

Traci's Story

Billy Beuthel and I grew up together in the mountains of Colorado up a valley called Deer Creek. From my childhood on, every summer Billy and I ran up and down the mountainside like wild coyotes. As adults, our paths took us in different directions. Decades went by and in the summer of 1999 our families were reunited. Both sets of parents had died. The Beuthel's had two children; we had four. Billy had become Bill and my hair had started turning gray but it almost seemed as if the many years had never passed.

Bill and Jan Beuthel's daughter Traci had been born with Rubenstein-Taybi syndrome. One in a hundred million have this problem, which creates retardation. At age 20, she functioned on a first- or second-grade level. It is difficult to have any idea what Traci is really thinking but the Beuthel's have given her every opportunity possible. Everyone loves Traci because she is such a gentle, thoughtful child with a distinctly soft voice.

On July 21, 2005, Jan's father, Howard Reid, died. I always called him Captain Reid because he had been an airline pilot for decades and once flew me over the mountains around Dear Creek in a one-engine airplane (Howard was 90 at the time). When the end came, we felt deep concern for the entire family. After Howard died and the funeral home came to pick up the body, the officials asked about taking his shoes. They informed the family that in death, the feet swell and it is impossible to get shoes on. The shoes could be placed in the casket but it was up to the family. Jan and her mother decided not to send them. The Captain would only have his socks on. It was a private conversation just between the two women and that was the end of the matter.

During this time, Traci was away at a summer camp. She didn't even know that her grandfather had died until she later returned home. Of course, nothing was said about the shoes and Traci wouldn't have understood the issue anyway. When the family went to the funeral home, Traci was uncomfortable and didn't want to get close to the body. She had never seen a dead person and didn't know how to handle her grandfather's immobile state. Jan tried to explain that she shouldn't be afraid. About a half-hour later, Traci came up to the casket and began stroking Howard Reid's hand. Jan could see that her daughter was talking to her grandfather and everything seemed to be okay. Of course, Jan was relieved to find things working out. She walked over to the casket where Traci was quietly talking to Mr. Reid.

"Everything is fine?" Jan asked.

Traci turned around and said softly. "Grandpa is okay and he is wearing shoes now." Traci walked away without any idea of what she had just said.

Despite her limitations, it appeared as if Traci Beuthel had received a message that her grandfather was well taken care of. She had the ability to neither anticipate nor understand such a communiqué. How could such a thing happen? This is one of those loose ends that are nearly impossible to explain or fit into a category that we've discussed so far in this book.

Norman's Story

Rev. Norman Neaves had been an Oklahoma boy with deep family roots in the state's history. When he was two or three years old, his family lived on a farm northwest of Chickasha as home-steaders. His grandfather died in August, a murderously hot month in Oklahoma, and a wake was held. Norman's mother had been upset because she worried that her father wasn't the religious person she thought he should have been. That night she slept next to an open window with no screen, worrying about her father's fate. Something unusual happened that she did not tell Norman about until years later when he told her that he was going into the ministry.

"Norman, I'm telling you this because I haven't told any-body lest they think I was hallucinating." She shook her finger emphatically in his face. "But I wasn't hallucinating or seeing things. I know that this story is true."

Norman leaned closer to get her details.

"That night of the wake, I couldn't go to sleep because I was worried. I was really upset. I just didn't know what to think. At that moment in the middle of the night, a turtledove flew down and landed on my window sill. Bathed in the light of the full moon, the bird sat there and cooed like a pet. He didn't fly off and wasn't afraid. I felt a wonderful sense of presence as though that bird represented an angel . . . or . . . maybe in some way . . . my father. The bird stayed there for the longest time until finally it flew away into the light and disappeared."

Norman stared at his mother in consternation.

"I was wide awake and it really happened. Now that you're going into the ministry, I wanted to share the story with you."

The years passed, Norman's ministry flourished, and in 1999, he and his wife, Kip, took a group of people on a Holy Land Tour that ended in the Garden Tomb in Jerusalem.

As the group gathered at the tomb, Norman delivered a short sermon to prepare them for receiving Holy Communion. In this sermon, he told the story of his mother's experience with the dove from decades long past.

Norman watched the crowd and was surprised that people started weeping while he was talking. Men started crying. Norman reflected that the story was important personally but never would have expected such a response from his group. As he served Communion, people reached out and squeezed his hand. Their continuing emotion left him mystified.

After the service concluded with the Lord's Prayer, congregants rushed forward. Gary Dage was in this group. Standing with him were Jerry Gamble and Jayne Jayroe, both crying. Obviously, the entire group was still moved.

Jerry said to Norman, "While you were preaching, you weren't aware of what was happening behind you?"

"No, I wasn't." Norman shook his head.

"Behind you was a branch sticking out of the tree and two turtle doves landed on the branch." Jerry said. "The doves sat there the entire time you were telling your mother's story. They cooed back and forth. At one point, you gestured and the doves flew up a little higher but they stayed right there. They remained the entire time."

"When we opened our eyes after the final prayer, they were gone," Gary Dage added.

The group's Orthodox Jewish tour guide had now come forward with tears in his eyes as well. "Norman," he said, "that's right! They were turtle doves but we *don't have* turtle doves in Israel."

Two doves. One for Norman's grandfather? One for Norman's mother? Who can say?

It's a loose end that doesn't seem to fit but what a beautiful loose end it is! Such stories certainly push us to consider mysteries outside the scope of what we've seen so far, and beg for deeper and broader understanding.

Conclusion

Who can explain these small pieces that don't fit the patterns we've seen in our journey so far? There may be contradictions and inconsistencies. I find that it's important not to let what I can't explain make me doubt what I know. When it's all said and done, the issue remains one of faith. It is what we believe to be true that counts with each of us. Time will clarify the final issues and the pieces that don't fit.

Touching the Heart of God

The introduction to this book suggested these pages would help you in dealing with the reality of death. The desire was to change your natural fear of the inevitable reality into a posture of confidence. I told you that I believe a dignified celebration of death is possible. Rather than hiding from the Valley of the Shadow, the snapshots have hopefully given you the courage to look at your own death even more constructively. Along the way, I noted that this promise is not based on a person's story but comes through faith in the resurrection of Jesus Christ from the dead. Of course, it is *all* a matter of faith.

However, faith does not stand alone. Recently, Pope Benedict had an explosive confrontation with Islamism following a speech in which he was attempting to clarify how important it is to keep faith and reason together. His insightful lesson got lost when he referenced early Islam's attempts to convert people by the edge of a sword (remarks that were met with rioting in several Muslim countries). The pope was making an important point for the entire world: The modern scientific world must not lose faith. At the same time, communities of faith must not forget the importance of reason. Modern science has given the world great achievements. On the other hand, when faith doesn't use reason, the result is a blind faith that turns into fanaticism.[1]

I find that we have to react to these snapshots from near-death moments with a combination of faith and reason. The stories can't be proved, which makes them a matter of faith. Yet, when we read them, hear them and think about them, they become evidence, albeit anecdotal, and that makes them also matters of reason. I believe that the album of snapshots we've been inspecting can give us certainty and expectation as we approach the end of our own lives. As Gary Dage discovered and proclaimed, dying is walking from one world into the next with such ease that we don't know when we died. I find his confidence reflected in these experiences offered to us by a multitude of friends and saints. Let's explore how these experiences can also take us to the heart of God.

I. Near-Death Experiences Offer Hope

During a Quantum Mind Conference in Tucson in March 2003, Dr. Pim van Lommel shared some of his thoughts during an interview. Trained as a cardiologist, Dr. van Lommel currently studies near-death events full time. His research indicates that 18 percent of the people who died of cardiac arrest and were resuscitated had a near-death experience of some variety. Five percent had a highly significant encounter. Dr. van Lommel has considered this issue with the same concern and careful attention that he uses in his normal field of medicine. Because he understands what has occurred during near-death episodes, other patients can talk to him with confidence. He has many stories to tell and here's one of them.

After having a heart attack, a man was brought into the hospital cyanotic (blue) from lack of oxygen and was unconscious. In trying to help the unconscious man, the nurse had to remove his dentures and put them on the crash cart before they could intubate him. For 90 minutes, the staff labored over the patient, attempting to restore blood pressure and create heart rhythm. If the person can be restored in the first 5 to 10 minutes, he can return to normal functioning. However, when the treatment is drawn out and there is a lack of oxygen, the result is a functional loss in the brain, creating permanent damage. After a week, this patient remained in a deep coma without any reflexes. Obviously, the damage had been highly significant.

A week later, the same nurse who attended the man when he entered the hospital came into his room to administer medication. The man suddenly opened his eyes and said, "Oh, you're the one who took my dentures out and put them in the drawer in that funny cart."

The nurse was so flabbergasted that she nearly had her own near-death experience. The patient continued talking and described the people standing around in the room while she was working. The nurse couldn't believe her ears. The patient said, "I was desperately trying to contact you to say, 'Please go on, because if you stop trying to help me, I will die.'"

Dr. Pim van Lommel related that the unconscious man could not only perceive what was happening but he also clearly heard everything, even though he was in a comatose state. How does such a story strike you? It gives me hope and encouragement. When I observe the recovery and regeneration of a person, it gives me even more added confidence.

2. Glimpses of Eternity Offer Personal Encouragement

Everyone wonders and worries about what will happen when they die. We naturally feel apprehension about what must be out there beyond our last breath. While near-death stories start at different points, they universally give us reassurance that we don't need to worry.

Rev. Ed Foust was an Air Force chaplain before he started hospice work. A minister in the Baptist Church, Ed was working in a hospital in the Midwest when he was confronted with a difficult situation. Three-year-old Pat had developed leukemia and nothing seemed to be halting the disease. Ed dropped by to visit with the boy's father, pray with the child and attempt to console the family. Pat was dying, but strangely he kept pointing toward a corner of the room as if someone was standing there.

Ed knew the boy's death would be a challenge to his abilities, so he took a careful look at what was happening in the room. The father had just gotten up out of a chair to help his son. Pat was saying something but was so quiet that it was impossible to hear. The father bent down and put his ear near his son's mouth. Ed could see the child's lips moving. For a moment the father listened and then suddenly straightened. His face had turned sheet-white, and he stared at the boy. Ed moved closer to the man.

"What's he saying?" Foust asked.

"He's saying, 'Grandpa! Grandpa!'" the father whispered.

"Interesting," Ed replied thoughtfully.

"Yes." The father's voice quivered. "His grandfather died five years ago and he's never met him."

The next day, Pat died.

What do you make of a child who recognizes a grandfather he's never met, a grandfather who silently stands in the corner waiting to help the boy cross into eternity? I find that scene to be highly reassuring and comforting. I have sat with many good people as the life drained out of them. Those last moments can become difficult, bleak and are usually quiet or may be filled with an occasional moan. But the realization that there is a possibility that we have someone standing by, waiting for us, waiting to offer a hand, gives us encouragement so that we can face death without apprehension.

3. The Accounts Produce Greater Personal Growth

Periodically, some experience comes along that causes us to stop and reconsider our approach to reality. Is it as solid as we thought? Often, books or movies challenge us to look beyond our regular thought patterns, culture or experience. When we attempt to understand other perspectives, thought patterns or cultures, we grow. My excursions into the near-death world have expanded how I discern reality. Let me explain with one of these stories.

Rev. Ray Wade had been a preacher with the Pentecostal Holiness Church before he became a chaplain with a hospice group. One of his patients was a woman whose father had been a circuit rider with the Nazarene Church many years before. In her late 80s, she was neither a Nazarene nor a Methodist. She just said that she loved Jesus and that was enough. Her sense

of humor never left and fortunately she didn't experience pain that devoured so many people. Cancer had sickened her body and her time was short when Wade came into her room.

The chaplain came by and she explained that she had been visiting with her sister. Wade knew the sister had been dead for years. She went on to say she was also visiting with her husband.

"He's over there in that chair. I want you to meet him." She raised up and looked toward the wall. "Oh, I guess he went down to the cellar but I do want you to know him."

Chaplain Wade did not think she was hallucinating. He told me that he believed that "she had on a different set of glasses that we can't wear." His phrase has stuck with me. *A different set of glasses.* I find that colloquialism to be a good way to express the shift that happens with the dying. The chaplain had no doubt that the woman was lucid and not out of touch with reality. She simply had objects in sharp focus that we can't see.

Think about it. Could these stories possibly challenge you to greater growth or change your current perspective of death?

4. These Accounts Put Us in Touch with God

The Scriptures proclaim that the power of God is available to do great things in our lives. However, often we don't begin to access the potency of God's power until we are in a bind. When we hit the wall, we are far more apt to consider this great promise. The Bible says, "For the grace of God that brings salvation has appeared to all men . . . the blessed hope and glorious appearing of our great God and Savior Jesus Christ, who gave Himself for us, that He might redeem us" (Titus 2:11,14).

The word "redemption," related to the Greek word *lutron*, implies a "releasing," as might have occurred when a slave was bought out of bondage. *Lutron* was a price paid for deliverance. Only when people have been in some form of captivity can they fully appreciate the promise of freedom. Prisoners instantly understand. People who have nearly died also understand! They understand how tightly the door of death can be locked. When we stand at that last door, we will know that only the power of God can provide redemption.

I know because I've been there myself.

I came face to face with death when I was 31 years old. Each year in the fall, I suffered from a severe attack of allergies. Expecting it to hit me like a truck, I went on about my business even when the sneezing, red eyes, and sore throat developed. On this particular fall, the winds were significantly hot, and before long I developed a piercing back pain, with accompanying elevation of temperature. I felt terrible but kept working as usual. On Sunday morning, I preached away, called for the offering, and hoped my flushed face might prompt a heart-felt response from the congregation.

After the second week of a constant temperature, a doctor in the congregation came up to me and noted that an enduring temperature was an important call to examination. Dr. Charles Harvey was an excellent internist and said I needed to come in and see him. I reluctantly agreed and kept on working. Actually, I took what he said lightly and didn't give it the weight I should have. On Tuesday, I went to his office and he began testing. As soon as the appointment was through, of course, I went back to my office to keep on working.

Dr. Harvey called late that afternoon to tell me that I hadn't listened to him but the time had come for me to pay careful attention. My allergic reactions had given rise to a secondary infection. Consequently, I had developed acute nephritis, an inflammation of the kidneys in a parenchyma condition, meaning the whole organ had become diseased. Dr. Harvey expressed concern that my kidneys might start shrinking. At the time, I didn't understand how serious this was, but Dr. Harvey convinced me that I needed to go home and go to bed.

Almost immediately the condition escalated and soon I was sleeping 20 hours a day. I began to develop double-vision and could no longer read. My back hurt terribly and nothing brought relief. Dr. Harvey explained that because it was a secondary infection, the problem was difficult to treat. Uremic poisoning remained a possibility. Talk began to circulate about dialysis, which wasn't all that common in those days. Finally, Dr. Harvey suggested that I go to St. Anthony's Hospital for a dye test to give the doctors an inner look at what was happening in my kidneys. He warned me the test would cause burning, which was painful.

The technicians wheeled me in on a gurney and stuck the needle in my vein. It felt like they were pouring liquid fire into my arm. I needed something to distract me from the pain. When I looked up at the wall, I noticed a large crucifix (it was a Roman Catholic hospital). I decided to focus my attention on the suffering of Christ and try to identify with the awful struggle He endured on the cross, in hopes it would get my mind off my pain. I hadn't heard of anyone doing such a thing. To my surprise, I found that my discomfort eased some. The more I attempted to identify with what had happened to Jesus Christ, the more my suffering seemed to lessen. At least, I didn't hurt as badly as before. By the time they finished the X-rays, I had become so absorbed in this meditation that I hardly noticed it was over. While my wife drove me home, I sat in the car lost in my thoughts. The incident had been surprising.

During the next several days, my conditioned worsened. Finally, one afternoon I awoke to discover that my wife had placed a large open book on the nightstand while I was sleeping. It looked like an encyclopedia. Seeing double, it was hard to read but I discovered that she had gone to the library and picked up a medical book describing my situation. As I read what she had outlined in pencil, I realized I *was dying*.

The awareness that I would not live much longer did not frighten me because my Christian faith had already promised me eternal life, but I sensed complete isolation. I felt the lonely awareness of watching a parade go down the street and disappear around the corner while I stood by myself. My children would grow up but I wouldn't be there. Someone else would walk my daughter down the aisle when she got married. The lights were off in my bedroom and darkness settled over me. I felt empty.

I didn't want to die.

Never had I heard anyone seriously talk about divine intervention or healing. I could not see any hope—not until I remembered that crucifix at St. Anthony's hospital.

Certainly something important had happened to me when I was lying on that X-ray table. *Maybe seeing the suffering figure of Christ had accomplished something,* I thought. *Possibly, I should try to return to that same place again.* My mind began to fill with

Bible passages that I had memorized several years earlier. From the book of Isaiah came the words, "Surely He has borne our griefs and carried our sorrows; yet we esteemed Him stricken, smitten by God, and afflicted. But He was wounded for our transgressions . . . the chastisement for our peace was upon Him, and by His stripes we were healed" (53:4-5).

The words rolled around in my head over and over. Abruptly, a verse from the New Testament came from out of nowhere: "By whose stripes you were healed" (1 Pet. 2:24). I stretched my arms out and softly said over and over, "Jesus, Jesus, Jesus." My imagination created a scene. I could see Jesus Christ on the cross just like I had seen in the crucifix on the wall. It was as if I were standing before the cross in A.D. 33, looking up at Jesus stretched out in the same way I was in the bed. Suddenly, I was on the cross with Christ. I was in Christ and Christ was in me.

Words from the New Testament surged through my mind: "I have been crucified with Christ; it is no longer I who live, but Christ lives in me; and the life which I now live in the flesh I live by faith in the Son of God, who loved me and gave Himself for me" (Gal. 2:20). It was as if both Robert Wise and Jesus Christ were dying together and yet, at the same time, I was alive in Christ more than I had ever been alive in my life. I have no idea how long I stayed suspended in thought and lost in His love.

Slowly, the scene faded from my mind, but I didn't open my eyes. Without moving, I rested in the awareness that something awesome had occurred beyond anything I could ever have dreamed. At that moment, I felt light beginning to fill the bedroom. I kept my eyes closed but the light became so bright that I had to squint. It felt like I was out on a beach with summer sunlight flooding over my body, bathing me with vitality. I could literally feel the increase in warmth in the room, and in me. My body felt like it was being wrapped in light but it was also penetrating to the core of my being.

I can't tell you whether this lasted for minutes or hours. Finally, I drifted off to sleep. Usually, I slept around the clock until the next afternoon but I woke up the next morning at around 10:00. I was startled because I felt so good and refreshed. Where it had become difficult for me to move, I seemed to be quite flexible. On the nightstand was one of my books, which I picked up. To my delight, I wasn't seeing double and started to read.

The phone rang.

"This Dr. Harvey's office," the nurse said. "I'm sorry to wake you but the doctor wants to take a urine sample. We'll send somebody by in a few minutes. Just wanted you to know."

I thanked the nurse and kept reading. I've always been a voracious reader and it seemed so good to be able to see clearly again. Shortly, the person came for the sample and I went back to reading. In about an hour, the phone rang again.

"This is Dr. Harvey's office again," the nurse said. "We've made some mistakes. We need to take another sample. I'm sorry to bother you but the person is on his way right now."

Without delay, the delivery person came, left again, and I got back to reading. It took me a while to fully understand that something had happened. At noon, I got up and went into the kitchen to fix some soup. I hadn't done that in so long that the realization began to settle in that I felt better than I had in weeks. About that time the phone rang again.

"This is Charles Harvey," the doctor said with some irritation in his voice. "You don't listen to me well anyway, but what's going on now? Is this a joke or something?"

"What?" I blinked several times.

"Are you sending tea over here?" Dr. Harvey asked with irritation in his voice.

"Are you kidding?" I protested. "I don't understand."

"Look!" Dr. Harvey said. "These urine samples are normal. No albumin, protein, nothing unusual. It can't be. The tests all indicate normality."

When I hung up the telephone, my mind was whirling. The doctor had said that I was well. It took me about six months to regain my normal stamina but I certainly wasn't dying anymore. And what about those shrinking kidneys? Once kidney tissue starts to shrink, the process is irreversible. Back in those days there were no kidney transplants. You tried to live on dialysis as long as you could. Today I've still got my kidneys. *I just got well.*

My story is not a near-death experience in that I did not step over the line beyond life as in the other stories. However, it was near-death in that I got close. Closer than I had ever wanted to get. I felt the emptiness of leaving this world behind and knew no human could do anything to stop it. The medical authorities tried but the illness exceeded their grasp. I believe I wouldn't have gotten out of the grip of disease if I had not been ransomed by the work of Christ on the cross.

Do I believe in the power of God to redeem? Can the cross of Jesus Christ pull us back from the edge? Absolutely. In the midst of death, nothing could ransom me from the end but that power.

5. The Snapshots Give Us Confidence in Our Convictions

It's one thing to sit in church and listen to a sermon promise us a checklist of possibilities. It's quite another matter to believe it's all true, especially when we're lying in bed surrounded by blackness at 2:00 in the morning.

Most of the time, we don't really hold our beliefs firmly until they have been tested by fire. After we've been dragged through an ordeal, then our ideals become enduring. In the first letter of Peter we are told, "For a little while, if need be, you have been grieved by various trials, that the genuineness of your faith, being much more precious than gold that perishes, though it is tested by fire, may be found to praise, honor and glory at the revelation of Jesus Christ" (1 Pet. 1:6-7). Only after the struggle has passed are we grateful for what was accomplished by the battle. Nevertheless, whatever turns our sense of confidence into enduring conviction is worth the conflict.

Here's an example.

I first met Cecil Henson when I was a teenager. My sister was dating his son and I found Cecil to be a fascinating man. He was brilliant, perceptive, but *different*. Hard to put my finger on how, but he seemed more perceptive than most of the people I knew. Mellow. Insightful. I didn't know exactly why but I knew Cecil had an unusual quality. One afternoon I learned the reason.

Cecil told me the story of what happened to him in 1941. When his son Van was born, Cecil's wife died during the birth, and he was so distraught that he could not even raise the baby himself. Van was placed in Cecil's sister's care while Cecil struggled. By 1941, Cecil had developed terrible stomach ulcers and had to undergo serious surgery. The operation didn't fare well and his physical body teetered on the edge of life. The incisions in his abdomen actually broke and his abdomen burst open, expelling his intestines on the bed. The small hospital caring for Cecil was ill-prepared for such trauma and his shock was overwhelming.

Cecil Henson died.

I was staggered when Cecil told me what happened *after* his demise. This was my first near-death story. Cecil described coming out of a blackness and emerging into another realm where a multitude of hands were extended to pull him up and out of the mire he had been caught in. Much later, Cecil discovered that many people were praying for him at that moment and he came to interpret those "hands" to be prayers.

After a series of experiences, Cecil came to a place where he had to decide whether he would stay in heaven or come back to Earth. The incredible peacefulness and sense of well-being that had come over him during this time made the decision difficult. At that moment, he encountered the risen Jesus Christ with His magnificent face radiating love and glowing with a wondrous light. Cecil stared in amazement and then the face began to change. He realized it was like pictures in the newspaper in those days. The shape and nuances of the face were determined by the shading in a thousand small dots. As he watched, the "dots" that defined the face of Christ began to increase in size and come forward. One of the dots started coming directly toward Cecil and he realized that it was actually *a face*, the face of a woman who had shown him kindness many years earlier. The woman's face receded and another "dot" came forward. In it was a man who had taught Cecil as a child in a Sunday School class. One by one, the circles kept coming forward and then withdrawing back into the face. Each circle was the face of a person who had shown Cecil kindness and unconditional love. He was astonished. The face of Christ was composed of a multitude of people who had shown Cecil gracious affection over the years.

In that moment, Cecil Henson knew he had to return to Earth and that one of his tasks was to help his son Van become a man. The amazing journey occurred while Cecil *was dead* . . . before he returned to tell the story to people like me.

After I listened to the entire experience, I understood why Cecil was different. Like other near-death survivors, he had no fear of death. And afterward, a gentle calm filled his life as he attempted to walk the path Christ had laid down.

His story certainly gave me new conviction.

Years later, I stood beside Cecil's bedside as he was dying. At that moment, all I could think about was the marvelous face of the Redeemer that was once again smiling down on Cecil.

The Bottom Line

I began this chapter with the observation that the confidence and conviction we need is basically a matter of faith and suggested that we need to put faith and reason together to get the maximum benefit of both. We have to pay attention to the directives and guidelines that come with the experience. If we don't pay attention, we miss the benefits; if we do pay attention, we receive the blessing. Here's a story that in its own unique way is a small parable about the promise.

When I was attending seminary, I had the opportunity to meet Dr. E. Stanley Jones. A medical doctor, Dr. Jones had a worldwide impact during the '40s and '50s when he was a missionary in India. A brilliant man, Dr. Jones's profound spirituality touched thousands in this country through the weeklong conferences he held, called "ashrams." I heard him tell this story.

Just as World War II began, Dr. Jones was in China when the Japanese began their invasion. He knew that if he didn't get out of China quickly, he would be there possibly for the entire war. Dr. Jones caught the last tramp freighter leaving China and piled his many possessions on board, knowing it would take him a long time to get back to India. The old ship wound its way slowly from port to port while Dr. Jones could only impatiently hope for the best. Winding around what is today called Vietnam and Thailand proved arduous. They had to get beyond Burma to finally arrive in India. However, it was Dr. Jones's practice not only to pray for protection but also to attempt to listen to what the Holy Spirit might say to him in return.

As the boat pulled into one of those out-of-the-way docks that no travel agency even sent its customers to visit, Dr. Jones prayed as usual. In his mind and heart, the voice of God spoke back.

"Get off the boat," the Holy Spirit said.

Dr. Jones blinked in bewilderment. To end up in this port was nearly as bad as to get stuck in China! He must have heard wrong.

"Get off this boat," the Holy Spirit repeated.

Because Dr. Jones did what he believed the Spirit of God told him to do, with the greatest reluctance, he had all of his possessions removed from the ship and piled on the dock. Standing in the midst of his goods, Dr. Jones watched the freighter sail out into the Andaman Sea. He felt like a fool and knew that his problem of returning to India had only deepened.

As he watched the boat sail a mile out into the harbor, a terrible roar echoed back to the shore as fire and smoke suddenly filled the air. A Japanese submarine had torpedoed the ship and it sank, killing all passengers.

When Dr. Jones told this story, a hand immediately shot up in the air. "Do you mean that you were the only person God was speaking to?" the man asked.

"No, sir," Dr. Jones snapped. "I was the only one listening."

Note

1. "Faith and Reason," *The International Jerusalem Post,* September 22-28, 2006, Jerusalem, Israel, p. 9.

Using the Pictures

"If anyone has ears to hear, let him hear."
And He said to them,
"Take heed what you hear."

MARK 4:23-24

The third section will focus on how we can help the dying based on clues from their snapshots of eternity. The pictures can better equip us to assist people in leaving this world and getting on their way to that City above all cities. I will attempt to show you how you can be of primary assistance in starting others in their journey. As astonishing as it sounds, each of us has the capacity to bring and convey life to the sick and dying. In order to make a significant difference, we must listen carefully to them. You will find some lessons in the following chapters. Increased awareness is needed.

Ears to Hear

Informed caregivers can develop an ability to minister that will give them the capacity to make a significant difference. One of the first steps is to develop a listening presence that hears at all levels what the dying person might be communicating. For many people, this proves to be a difficult task. People with strong Christian convictions at any place along the theological spectrum may find themselves placed in uncomfortable positions. Listening demands searching for the other person's meaning. The bottom line is that we have to put the patient's needs ahead of our own.

Share the Faith

One of the most helpful aspects of bringing peace to the dying is assisting them to discover their destiny. Many people come to the end of their lives with no sense of destiny. They have not been around the Church or heard the Christian message in a way that made sense to them. Time drifted by and one day the ultimate end came into view. What could they cling to?

Many non-Christians generally accept the Bible as an ultimate source of meaning and truth. I've found that when someone inquires about what is on the other side of death that he or she pays close attention to what is in Scripture. Being able to open a Bible and point out scriptural promises in their proper context can make a dramatic difference. Chaplains and people who work with the dying often memorize verses that help make the promise of eternal life clear. Many children memorized John 3:16 when they were young. If a person memorizes John 3:16, then perhaps he or she will recall that verse at a time near the end of life and offer great hope to a dying friend or relative. In fact, the entire third chapter of John's Gospel is a powerful statement of the gift Jesus Christ gave to the world. The chapter ends by saying, "He who believes in the Son *has* everlasting life" (John 3:36, emphasis added). Recalling these passages offers clarity and direction.

In chapter 4, we noted the theme that John developed in his first letter: "This is the testimony: that God has given us eternal life, and this life is in His Son. He who has the Son has life" (1 John 5:11-12). A promise that extends across 2,000 years and lands by the bedside of the dying has the capacity to shore up dwindling hopes and bring a wonderful sense of confidence that God has planned a wonderful future beyond death. I have shared these passages with the folks at the end of their life's journey and watched the light come on in their eyes.

A similar set of promises and explanations comes from Paul's letter to the Romans. The apostle explained how the death of Jesus Christ covered the issues in our lives that worry us and create doubt. Often called "The Roman Road," each of these verses explains an important aspect of the recovery that has been offered to each of us. For example, Romans 3:23 explains that no one is exempted from coming short of what God wanted them to be. Romans 6:23 details the penalty that we naturally feel deep within us but also turns our attention to the gift of life God desires for us. Reading Romans 5:8 offers assurance that His gift of accepting love has already been extended because Jesus Christ died for each of us. Finally, Romans 8:31-35 offers the absolute certainty that nothing can separate us from God's gracious gift.

Putting this biblical story into our own words and sharing it with the dying can bring them back from despondency and bewilderment. As I have prayed with people during such moments of despair, I have watched the good news reverse their outlook. Such an about-face is never as critical as when someone is standing at death's door. My experience has been that the best approach is gently following where their questions lead while explaining the message in the same way that one might discuss alternatives on the supper menu. The task isn't to impose a viewpoint but to help them answer their questions. Dropping a "turn or burn" message on them is usually about as constructive as bombing houses to encourage peace! The whole ministry process begins by listening carefully before we speak.

Nurse Patricia Ackerson discovered how important it is to help people spiritually cross the line between life and death with a deep sense of spiritual confidence. While we were discussing her work with the dying, Patricia told me she has found that many people have more control over the timing of the end of their lives than we might think. The exact moment they depart is often shaped by how ready they are spiritually. She recognized that while the Bible indicates that all our days are written down in His book, it doesn't say anything about the hours. The last few moments may be far more in our hands than we realize.

One of Patricia's clients had been in a coma for a considerable amount of time with her family standing around expecting the end to be imminent. However, the patient kept hanging on. Somewhere out there on the highways of America, the patient had a wayward son whom she had not seen for a long time and she longed for a reunion with him. A number of professionals and relatives stood around the woman's bed as the clock ticked away. Abruptly, the son came roaring in from California on his black motorcycle and walked into the room. Twenty minutes later, the lady died. The family and friends believed she was delaying her demise until this reconciliation occurred.

Because of experiences like this one, Patricia Ackerson began helping lingering patients with a special prayer. She would place her hand on the patient's forehead and pray a biblical benediction: "May the Lord bless you and keep you, may He make His face to shine about you, and be gracious unto you. May He lift up the light of His countenance upon you and give you peace. Now and forever, Amen." This form of sharing our faith offers great encouragement to uncertain people at critical times. Those actions that arise out of our convictions and aid someone in going forward without fear of abandonment can be immensely helpful. Such words and actions encourage the dying that their lives can stop without fear so that they can relax and let go.

Listening to the Dying

The most important act we can engage in when a person lays on his or her deathbed is simply to make ourselves available to listen.

Do we have enough respect to take the person seriously and to hear his or her dying words? Do we take the experiences and stories of the dying as important as they attempt to speak? While it would seem obvious that we would take a dying person seriously, this is not always the case. Often, observers are more likely to discount the dying and carry on a conversation around the person as if the patient can't hear or understand what is being said.

Such an approach can leave a patient feeling misunderstood and alone. The patient usually wants to be taken seriously and is bothered or saddened when discounted. At the bedside of someone who is dying, we need to listen with the same intensity we would give any person talking to us in normal conversation, perhaps more. We must assume what they are saying is valid rather than tossing it aside without examination. This is true whether the dying are speaking in gibberish, trying to convey some last advice, or just talking to a person about the weather.

Rev. Rick Haug, a Pentecostal Holiness minister and hospice chaplain, shared Eva's story with me. Throughout her life, Eva had been a devout Roman Catholic, but by the time she was 90 years old, virtually everyone in her family was gone and she appreciated Rick's concern for her because there was no one else around. As the end approached, Eva would fixate on the corner of the room. She would quietly call the names of family members who had passed as if they were standing there or waiting just beyond the wall. From time to time, Eva would reach out as if taking someone by the hand. For three days, she continued on this level of intense conversation with the unseen. Eva shared with Rick that on one occasion she had seen the Lord Jesus Christ, leaving her with a profound memory of the experience.

Rick stayed by her and witnessed this happening with his eyes and ears. He listened to her on her deathbed and perhaps helped to make her death a little bit more hopeful and peaceful.

Consider Carefully What You Hear

"Consider carefully what you hear," Jesus told us (Mark 4:24, *NIV*). Pondering the snapshots of eternity with our eyes can help us hear well with our ears. In this chapter, we've discussed how to share and encourage the dying, while also listening to whatever it is they want to communicate to us, or to the world. Our response must come from a place of love, compassion and hope, and, above all, we must rest with them with great patience. The dying need this emotional, psychological and spiritual support. Offering this kind of support, I believe, is an example of considering carefully what we hear. While doing research for this book, I met with a group of chaplains from Preferred Hospice in Oklahoma City and learned another lesson about how important it is to listen to those patients we might think are hallucinating. These chaplains made the point that the families of the dying usually know the dying patients well and can tell when they are and are not hallucinating. Family members are keenly aware if their relatives are on a drug causing a delusional experience.

In all their experience, not one of these six chaplains had ever had a family member negate the snapshots their dying relative offered. In fact, the chaplains told me that these near-death spiritual responses shouldn't be negated because they aren't like other types of responses. The snapshots come from a different unearthly place, and it was their opinion that they should be taken seriously.

This is nothing if not great affirmation that we must stay keenly attuned to what the dying have to say. Even if it sounds like nonsense to our rational, modern ears, we must still learn to be patient listeners. Let us listen closely and consider carefully what we hear!

Near-Death Awareness

Charlotte Lankard is a well-known marriage and family therapist and has been a columnist in Oklahoma City for a number of years. She introduced me to her cousin Gary Lower because she wanted me to know the story of his mother's death. A man's man, Gary Lower had been a track coach at the University of Oklahoma as well as a recruiter for the football program at the school. For 23 years, he worked for the Fellowship of Christian Athletes, and Gary understood the meaning of death because he had had a severe heart attack at age 56. The encouragement of his daughter Regina had given him the stamina to stay alive. Today, Gary is 70 and going strong.

Trudy, Gary's mother, went blind soon after entering a nursing home. Macular degeneration kept narrowing her eyesight but it didn't slow the godly, self-determined woman down a notch. A good Baptist, she had come from a family of 12 who lived through the Great Depression and the Oklahoma Dust Bowl days and they endured every hard time with determination.

Every opportunity Gary had, he went to see his mother to tell her how much he loved her. In time, Gary began to recognize that his mother was weakening significantly and he knew the end wouldn't be far away. At about this time, Trudy began experiencing visits from her brothers and sisters. Although she was physically blind, she could see each of her visitors as clearly as Gary saw the wallpaper. He was pleased that these strange appearances were so real (regardless of what they meant) because they encouraged his mother. Nothing deterred Trudy's awareness of what was going on around her.

"Dad came by last night," Trudy told Gary one evening. "He wore that little hat of his and his usual blue leisure suit." Trudy kept describing her deceased husband wearing what he had always worn in life.

"What did you talk about?" Gary asked.

"Oh, you know your dad! Hardly ever said much. Pretty quiet, you know. Just talked a little and then he was gone."

Over the next few days, Trudy's Aunt Nanny and Aunt Bee came by for a visit, and because they had all been such a close-knit family, her brothers and sisters also stopped in. On one occasion, Trudy got upset because she saw her sister walking down the hall but the nurses wouldn't let her go with her sister and Trudy became rather agitated about this delay. After all, they were family!

The end came peacefully. Trudy took a quiet breath and was gone.

Near-Death Awareness

One of society's problems has been that many people who have had such experiences have not shared them because of the fear that they might be thought deranged, or at best not taken seriously. Hopefully, this book will sensitize readers to the need to listen carefully as the end approaches. Listening carefully begins by paying attention *to everything* they say.

Trudy's story adds another dimension to our discussion. In addition to near-death experiences, Trudy had a kind of *near-death awareness*. This designation describes how the dying communicate what happens as their lives run down. We've seen several stories in this book about people who experience this kind of near-death awareness prior to death. As mentioned in the last chapter, hospice chaplain Ray Wade expressed it well: "They have on a different set of glasses than we wear." They haven't crossed back and forth over the line as John Faulk did when he returned to his father's and mother's bedside, but it's as if they've gained a form of enhanced vision or insight that allows them to see through the curtain dividing life and death.

Actually, such vision is not entirely beyond the scope of modern science. While we assume the hues on the color wheel are all there is to see, there are actually many more colors we don't have the capacity to see. A rainbow reveals a widely known spectrum of beautiful colors, but the world of color is much broader. Our eyes simply aren't equipped for picking up these unknown shades. Apparently, the same is true for what occurs at the edge of life. We simply haven't developed the capacity or the awareness to see these complex dimensions.

Although blind, Trudy Lower's inner eyes saw more than we can with retinas in excellent condition. In her hospital room, she was not alone. As many people approach death, they see similar things. Deceased friends, relatives and occasionally they even see Jesus. No one seems to see dinosaurs, alligators, a pack of wild dogs or random people they don't know. The encounters come out of the person's life and are validated by their past. All of these people seeing family members, or seeing things that we can't, is a form of near-death awareness that we see manifest in the dying.

Rev. Don and Joann Johnson had been friends of mine for decades and we had shared ministry over the years. When I heard Joann was dying, I was shocked and went to their house for a final visit. Just a few hours before her death, the hospice workers were helping her get back in bed. Joann paused to take off her wedding rings and hand them to Don.

"I don't think I'll be needing them anymore," Joann said calmly.

As the final moments came, Joann began looking around the room as if she were seeing something others had missed. She kept looking up the wall as if there was something beyond the wall that was coming into focus and she started to reach out her arms. I find this to be another example of a kind of *near-death awareness*. Joann hadn't crossed over but she was beginning to see the other side.

From Out of the Past

The introduction of this book began with World War I survivor Jack Oscar's story of observing his fellow dying soldier's experience of seeing his mother moments before his death on the battlefield. This encounter would be another example of a near-death awareness event. History is filled with these stories, although many are not well-known, and these stories add to our collection of experiences, all of which can sharpen our listening skills.

Such a story came from the life of Frederic Chopin, the great Polish composer and pianist. Just past midnight on October 17, 1849, Chopin stood at death's door. His life had been filled with ups and downs but no one doubted the extraordinary capacity of this sensitive man to create magnificent music. The doctor stood at his bedside ready to do whatever was possible to assist the musical genius in his final moments. Abruptly, Frederic Chopin awoke from deep sleep and shouted, "Mother, my poor mother!"

The doctor moved closer to help. "Are you in pain?"

"No more," Chopin said and died immediately.

No one was able to ask Chopin what he saw or if he had communicated with his mother because his death came so quickly.[1] However, it seems clear that he had moved into a kind of near-death awareness event.

A similar story occurred with Serge Rachmaninoff in 1943. A pianist and composer like Chopin, Rachmaninoff immigrated from Russia and purchased a home in Beverly Hills, California. On March 28, his illness reached a crisis point and the great musician began slipping away. However, Rachmaninoff was certain that his music was being played from somewhere in the house. His friends standing around at his bedside assured him this was not the case. The composer would not relent and kept insisting he could hear the sounds. His friends adamantly denied this was the case, but Rachmaninoff continued to hear the music playing until he died.[2]

Were the sounds of one of his symphonies only in Rachmaninoff's head? Or was this part of a near-death awareness? Music was one of the supreme values in Rachmaninoff's life.

For him to hear it with clarity and certainty that someone in the house was playing his music could indicate something extraordinary was happening to him as his body died. The fact that his friends heard nothing pushes his experience into the category of near-death awareness.

The book of Hebrews tells us, "We are surrounded by so great a cloud of witnesses, let us lay aside every weight, and the sin which so easily ensnares us, and let us run with endurance the race that is set before us, looking unto Jesus, the author and finisher of our faith" (12:1-2). The Christian community has always affirmed that this "great cloud of witnesses" surrounds us through our lives and on into eternity. The Apostle's Creed calls it *the Communion of the Saints*. This idea sounds similar to the idea that we meet with this cloud of witnesses upon our deaths.

The picture we receive from near-death awareness is that in the final moments of life, many people begin to see these realities start to appear around them. Those who are standing around the bed of the dying are given the opportunity to acknowledge and even witness one part of what is apparently quite clear to the departing.

How do we honor this increased awareness in a way that does not diminish the dying or what is happening with them? The Bible tells us that faith, hope and love abide but the greatest of these is love. I believe we can best express love in these moments by treating their statements, what they see or hear or any of their expressions, with honor and respect. Paying close attention to their heightened awareness is reassuring to them. As we take the dying seriously, they know they are being heard and that is comforting.

Notes

1. Scott Slater and Alec Solomita, *Exits: Stories of Dying Moments and Parting Words* (New York: Dutton, l980), p. 19.
2. Milton Cross and David Ewen, *Encyclopedia of the Great Composers and Their Music* (Garden City, NY: Doubleday, 1962), p. 603.

Helping the Living and the Dying

Assisting people dealing with the reality of death also means being aware of the needs of the living who stand by their dear ones as they slip away. As we read these snapshots, we realize that as people die, they turn their attention away from the living, even those they have loved dearly, and they turn to lock eyes with eternity. In the last chapter, we observed the story of Joann Johnson giving her rings back to her husband, Don, and saying factually, "I don't think I will be needing them anymore." While this could seem like a difficult moment, Joann directed her attention toward eternity. All of the near-death experiences we've considered were singular journeys. In the same way, we will travel across the threshold alone.

This certainly doesn't imply that the dying have become narcissistic in any way, rather that dying is a personal affair. We come into the world alone and we go out the same way. Those left behind who cared for the deceased will inevitably weep and experience loneliness when the departed start the next phase of their lives in heaven. Like a boy going to his first professional football game or his sister walking into a Disneyland toy shop, they can't help but be absorbed in what they are seeing around them rather than focusing on their loved ones. Unfortunately, the rest of the family sinks into shock.

And the trauma can be severe.

Joan Didion allowed the public to catch a glimpse of how harsh and rigorous the loss can be by opening her life to their scrutiny. Her best selling book *The Year of Magical Thinking* describes how quickly loss comes and how grief can swallow rationality without our knowing that the dragon's mouth has closed around our heads. Her book begins, "Life changes in the instant. The ordinary instant."[1] And how that instant can come at the snap of a finger! In 2003, the night before New Year's Eve, Joan Didion and her husband, John Gregory Dunne, sat down to supper after returning from the hospital where their daughter Quintana had been placed in an induced coma and was on life support. The couple had worked together for 40 years in a close, symbiotic partnership as two of America's outstanding writers. John was preparing to eat an evening meal when a massive fatal coronary ended his life. Joan Didion found him fallen from his chair and lying crumbled on the floor. The year of grief began what she called magical thinking.

Only in retrospect did Joan begin to recognize the contradictions in her thinking. At the time her various distorted thoughts and plans seemed as natural as the sun coming up. She continued to expect her husband to be right back after the doctor had pronounced him dead. She granted an autopsy because in some strange way it occurred to her that he might need such information when he returned for his things. On returning home from the hospital, Joan found her husband's coat dropped over a chair where he had placed it just before sitting down and dying. She absentmindedly mused that she needed to talk to him about leaving his jacket hanging about as well as several other matters involving his death (until she realized again that he was dead). It was one of those strange, magical moments.

Why is it that we do such things? The abruptness of death causes our minds to do cartwheels and we need someone to help us get back on our feet. A supportive friend can make a world of difference in how we regain stability and clarity of vision. Magical thinking sounds intriguing on paper but it's terrifying when it's sitting in the chair next to us. We can be of help to people struggling with these issues by listening constructively.

Listening Under Construction

The average person assumes that if he aims his mouth accurately then whatever comes out of it is going to make solid contact. While it's a good thought, communication is seldom as clear as we'd like it to be. During prolonged communication, the chances are good that it is probably going in the opposite direction. We generally don't stop to remember that everyone carries his own privately formed dictionary around in his head. The words are defined out of a person's experiences, the decades during which he or she grew up, and a thousand other nuances shaped by his or her life experiences, about which we know nothing. All this is to say that we must be attentive to whomever we're talking or listening.

For example, I once had a magnificent English sheepdog by the name of Chavis Regal that was as big as a small horse but as gentle as a lamb. Chavis had this strange habit of charging the front door whenever someone rang the bell. The beautiful dog meant nothing but a friendly greeting, although he sounded like a train roaring out of the living room. A friend dropped by once and rang our doorbell. Chavis bounded to the door like an attack of wild tigers. I walked up and saw the concerned look on the friend's face, staring through the glass door at this barking ball of fur. As a joke, I said to my friend that Chavis likes people, that he ate two last week. The man turned white!

What I didn't know was that the guy had been attacked by a tiny Chihuahua when he was three years old and gotten his chubby little legs chewed on. Because he was so small in those days, the dog looked to the child to be about the size of my sheepdog today. You get the picture. My joke didn't communicate humor, instead it simply left him terrified! I intended one thing; he heard another.

At that point, I needed a few lessons in the art of communication to help both of us get beyond a communication problem. Sometimes, we pick up these insights along the way and put them to good use, but just as often we don't. Here are a few pointers I believe can be extremely helpful in communicating with the dying and especially their families standing by.

1. Place Prior Verdicts About Near-Death Experiences on the Shelf
Religious people have a particularly hard time coming to the final moments without carrying an armload of preconditioned conclusions about near-death experiences along with them. Personal judgments have been with them most of their lives and they may even feel that each preconceived notion of what death

will be like is completely supported by the Bible. With these ideas firmly set in place, they approach the dying confidently and expect them to conform to their principles. Unfortunately, it doesn't usually work this way.

As we already noted, dying is an extremely personal matter. So when working with someone in this condition, we must accept who they are, and not expect them to be a certain way or other. The bottom line is that we should begin working with someone by opening our minds and leaving our own judgments behind. If something they say or do doesn't fit with our expectations, we must shift into their frame of reference and allow for it. My suggestion is to let go of your judgments and do your best to treat theirs with grace.

Persistent judgmental attitudes are often a sign than an individual has failed to confront his or her own issues. A judgmental attitude becomes a shield against having to deal with our own "stuff." Having worked in and around churches for years, I've observed that the most judgmental are often the most fearful. This is particularly true when it comes to death. In order to deal with the dying effectively, we must face our own mortality. Facing our own weakness puts us in a position to help others with theirs. If you can't hang your presuppositions on the wall and be accepting and nonjudgmental, you'd better take a hard look at them because they may be tripping you up.

2. Think Symbolically

We've already covered this area in several places, but it is important to consider that some of what the dying say can come in symbolic form.

By reiterating this, I want to make the point that we need to have a listening presence. Simply being with the dying can be an extraordinarily important task. Often, we can offer significant assistance by helping them recall old memories, if they feel comfortable thinking about this. Like going to the movies with someone, we can help them bring back stories that happened in their childhood, during the college years or at their first job. They may find that watching the movies in their head is preferable. Still, you can sit there at their side while the show goes on and offer support.

Sometimes the dying may want to write a letter to someone, and this addressee may be alive, or might in fact be someone who has already died. Being the secretary for such a need can be quite comforting for the dying person and highly informative. It may even be part of the symbolic experience that they're going through. Our task in this case is to help people put their feelings into a concrete form and release them.

3. Feedback

One of the techniques that counselors use is to take what they believe their clients have said and send it back to them in the form of paraphrased statements. Often, they will preface these statements with the phrase, "What I heard you saying was . . ." The client listens to the accuracy of what the counselor has reflected and is able to clarify the meaning so that genuine understanding develops. It often goes something like this:

The client shrieks, "I was so mad at my mother that I could have killed her."

"I hear you saying that you are really angry but do you mean that you wanted to murder your mother?" the counselor responds.

"No, no! I wouldn't physically hurt my mother but I was extremely upset."

"So you felt you could truly express your hostile feelings?" the counselor asks.

"No," the client says thoughtfully, "at least, not out loud. That's the problem; I could never tell my mother exactly what I was feeling."

Get the idea? Paraphrasing a person's words permits clarification and deeper understanding to follow until the full meaning emerges. By rephrasing statements that the dying make, we can help them to develop a clear sense that they are understood. In the same way, we are able to help the grieving find new direction.

This type of response develops when the listener asks leading questions that elicit a reply. Often, we are more prone to make assertions or statements that express our viewpoint. The dying might not do as well if we bombard them with our declarative statements (no matter how precious they are to us). Leading questions are more helpful because they draw the other person out. It's harder to come up with good, insightful and probing inquiries, but the results are far more productive.

4. Don't Be Afraid of Being Afraid

Fear of the unknown is normal and most people know less about death than anything else. Add to this all the fear generated by the images people see in horror movies, and the fear can be unbearable. Anyone coming to the end of his life journey will likely respond with feelings ranging from small anxieties to absolute terror. One of the reasons for writing this book is to offer examples of hope that can help individuals quiet their unavoidable sense of dread. Offering some of the examples from these chapters can help bring comfort and reassurance.

Do not be reluctant in extending words of comfort to your dear ones as they are preparing to step across a barrier that has already proved easy to cross. The folks who have been to the other side and come back most often report that they would never again be afraid of death. In fact, even though they are alive, they look forward to returning to the other side again. This book has been constructed to be like a photo album so that we can offer the collection of pictures to help them feel calm and reassured.

Naturally, many people fear the pain that can come with physical infirmity, disease and death. However, in today's world we are surrounded by a multitude of comforting medicines, procedures and medical techniques that offer an extraordinary level of assistance and freedom from pain. Nurses are trained to recognize needs quickly and respond immediately. We can assure the dying person that he or she doesn't need to be afraid of pain.

In fact as a person is close to death, what may sound like physical pain may not be physical discomfort at all. The day and night before Mitchell Brantley died, the family could hear him moaning and groaning as if he were in overwhelming pain. However, research has shown that often the dying make such noises and then awake to state they had no awareness of pain or hurting. These painful-sounding noises seem to be a kind of psychological wrestling with issues, problems or needs. We can hear these final sounds without being worried that the person is in physical agony. The groaning may be a part of the process of transformation as they move from their present state into eternity. While a sign of struggle, we don't necessarily need to worry that their agonizing sounds indicate pain for them.

5. Receiving a Final Accounting

One of the most powerful aspects of the Alcoholics Anonymous program of recovery is making the fifth step. After a struggling person completely surveys his entire life and faces every indiscretion, the individual comes to a person in confidence and tells every rotten thing that's ever happened to him, and every rotten thing he's ever done. In turn, the counseling listener helps the individual extend and receive forgiveness and achieve resolution of the past. During my years in the parish ministry, I heard many of these fifth-step confessions and discovered what a powerful release an individual can have in the process. I saw men and women set free of issues that had haunted them for decades simply by admitting the sin before God and another person.

Frequently, a dying person will have exactly the same need to confess to another person. Regardless of whether the behavior was scandalous or not, the individual feels the need to work through something he or she felt wasn't right. The problem isn't what they've done as much as it is the fact that they are still carrying or dragging it around with them. The time will come to dump that weight that's been on their back for ages. If you're the only person standing there or that they will talk to, it's important to listen. This is one of those moments when listening sensitively is of supreme importance (and don't forget that you must keep their confession confidential).

Remember, it's not your job to judge or make an assessment of the individual's life. Our job is simply to share that God offers His loving forgiveness. I often turn to 1 John 1:9 in the Bible and let them read it out of the Scripture for themselves: "If we confess our sins, He is faithful and just to forgive us our sins and to cleanse us from all unrighteousness." This seems to bring an even deeper sense of certainty that the past can be rectified. Our job is to help them understand this so that they can resolve their issues with their past (and with God) and get it behind them before they die.

When people have come to acceptance of all of the events in their life journeys, they will usually have an easier time dying well. Regardless of whether the past has been fair, unfair, happy or sad, they must be able to embrace and accept those old experiences in order to move across the final line with confidence. Often, we cannot help them do more than to know that a sympathetic ear is listening, but you'll probably find that this is usually enough.

Conclusion

We just reviewed how to help both the living and the dying through reserving judgment, listening, asking questions, giving feedback and even hearing out a person's confessions, when necessary. These are healthy things, as we can all use good feedback, encouragement or constructive listening from another person. And it always helps one to feel less alone when a friend gives us reason not to be afraid when we're shaking in our boots. By doing these simple things, you'll never know how much freedom and peace you can bring to another person.

A number of years ago, I had a prominent brain surgeon in my congregation. His wife came to me because she was concerned that her husband couldn't seem to get over his depression. Sam was even talking about leaving the field of medicine and she didn't know how to handle his problem. When I began talking with the neurologist, Sam told me that the death rate in his office was over 50 percent because most of his patients didn't come to him until their condition was beyond repair. Sam had seen too many people die and the weight of all these deaths was dragging him into this depression. As we talked over several sessions, I began to get a different picture of his faith than what he usually demonstrated on Sunday. Sam saw no hope for his patients when they died.

"When they die, they're dead," Sam said. "That's the end of it."

"You mean that you see no hope of anything beyond this world?" I asked.

Sam shrugged, "Of course not. When we're dead, the curtain drops. It's all over."

Much like I had done with parishioners in the hospital, I opened the Bible and began to talk with Sam about eternal life. We reviewed many of the passages that we've already considered in this book. Finally, Sam looked at me with consternation in his eyes.

"You mean that you *really* believe that when people die, there is a heaven?" Sam asked with genuine surprise.

"That's our faith," I said. "Haven't you heard that on Sunday mornings?"

"I thought we only said those words to make people feel good."

I'm sure that I looked surprised as I explained that we didn't run a dog and pony show selling some sort of elixir for the sick. The Bible was clear and the creeds confirmed the fact that for 2,000 years, Christians have firmly believed in going to heaven. Sam was amazed.

"When people die," I told him, "you are not sending them to a final dumping ground. You are part of helping them find their way to heaven."

Sam came to accept this biblical fact and didn't resign from his practice. He continued the extremely important tasks that he performed because he had found new hope. The last time we talked, Sam turned to me as he was leaving and said, "No one has ever talked to me like this before. Thank you."

Your job is to assist people in need to be able to say, "No one has ever listened to me like this before. Thank *you*."

Note

1. Joan Didion, *The Year of Magical Thinking* (New York: Alfred A. Knopf, 2005), p. 3

Healing

Snapshots from the dying also carry the veiled suggestion that we can offer more than we might think possible through our prayers for them. From what we see in the many experiences and stories we've read about, you too can be an agent of healing!

Healing someone who is dying? Come on!

Negative reactions like this to the suggestion of healing derive from the fact that we think of the word "healing" in a different way than it is generally used throughout Scripture. Our society usually considers that healing means the restoration of physical health. However, the Greek of the New Testament implies recovering wholeness of the entire person, which also includes emotional and spiritual well-being. *Therapeuo* can imply service to God as well as caring for or restoring someone. Often the biblical emphasis is on *restoration*. An individual with an amputation of a leg or arm can still be considered *a whole person*. In the same way, as individuals become physically weaker as death approaches, they are actually preparing to leave behind the bodily hindrances causing their demise.

From the stories that the dying who returned have told us, it is clear that they crossed the border line into eternity in a restored body of a different order. This metamorphosis seems to demonstrate restoration to the fullest extent possible. So if we use the word "healing" to imply full physical, emotional and spiritual restoration, then we will be closer to understanding how our prayers can be helpful. Is it possible to help the dying on this journey by praying? Absolutely.

Remember the story in chapter 1 of the two little boys who showed up beyond life at the same time trying to find their way into heaven? In this account the dying Al Harris had been trying to help create "a wind" to guide the children along. The first time I heard this story, I thought that Mr. Harris's attempts to assist the children had an unusual dimension. With more reflection, I found this aspect of his story offers a clue for us to follow. However, in order to put these pieces in the puzzle together, we need to discover more about the healings of Jesus along with His instructions to His followers to perform the same work. In addition, we will investigate what actually happens when we pray.

Restoration and Redemption

In chapter 15, I shared my personal story of struggling with death following the development of acute nephritis, which began to destroy my kidneys. While I obviously can't demonstrate the evidence, I do believe I would have died without divine intervention restoring my life. In my case, the word "restored" certainly fits the facts. Back in the late '60s, no one in the circles that I traveled in talked about or knew anything about this kind of healing. It was in a class with nonsense, and even praying for the sick was almost considered a form of emotional manipulation, a mind-over-matter phenomenon that likely passed as soon as the emotions wore off.

After my recovery, I realized that I had stumbled onto an aspect of the Christian faith that exceeded my wildest expectations. So I set out to study and understand what had happened to me. Much to my surprise, I found that many Christians across the centuries had been praying for the sick with profound results. Passages like James 5:13-15 that advised calling for the elders of the Church when someone was ill and having them pray and anoint with oil were not limited to the first century.

I now believe that the healing work of Christ didn't stop with the apostles but continued on with many godly people ministering healing through all of the past centuries. During the Medieval Age, such experiences were considered the work of the highly gifted with an aura of mystical aloofness surrounding the experience, but still, amazing events happened. Even the more skeptical period of the Enlightenment didn't stop these unique works of grace. I discovered that much of Church history was filled with these important restorations. Very few people had studied these events for direction in healing (at the time), partially because this form of ministry wasn't considered to be possible.

After all the study, I decided to attempt to offer healing in my local church. Once the service was announced, I was trapped. Even though I became increasingly apprehensive (since I'd never attended a healing service in my life), I had to go through with the experience because the congregation was waiting to see what would happen. That night I saw the first miraculous intervention of my life's ministry. June Watts, a dear friend and spiritual mother, experienced an extraordinary restoration in her ankles. Wanting to avoid any sort of reputation as a "healer," I avoided publicity that might sensationalize the ministry, but I continued praying for healing over the years. In time, I came to see that anyone could pray for the sick and accomplish significant results. Consequently, I began training people to pray in this way in the local church.

As various types of people became involved in training, I began to see that healing really wasn't particularly different from any other ministry. While anyone can pray for the sick, some people have highly significant results while others only see limited success. Some people have the possibilities of a far-reaching ministry but their friends only have occasional success.

Isn't this true of evangelism as well? Everyone can witness or reach out to others but they don't always get the same results. In every church there are a few people who bring a significant number of others to Christ. The same thing happens with Christian education. A few people prove to be great teachers, while their friends are only fill-ins. Healing ministry seems to operate according to the same formula. The bottom line is that I knew anyone can pray and make a difference in the lives of those with whom they pray.

When I applied these insights to the dying, I began to discover a new form of ministry. Usually, the final prayers are a form of dismissal, sending the person out of this world with God's blessing. Needless to say, such moments are precious and extremely helpful for the departing. They offer forgiveness, blessing and deliverance. However, I realized there was more to be done. I believe that the dying continue to need the peace and energy that comes with healing prayer.

With the passing years, I began to realize that praying for the sick is more than intervening for a specific problem. Actually, it is reaching out with one hand to touch the risen Christ while holding on to the sick with the other hand. Like reconnecting a broken electric power line, healing prayer is reestablishing contact with the Christ.

When Jesus said, "I am the way, the truth and the life," He was not only proclaiming a theological fact but also stating a physical truth. Jesus was *and is* the source of all vitality. John's Gospel begins with, "All things were made through him, and without him was not anything made that was made . . . to all who received him, who believed in his name, he gave *power* to become children of God" (John 1:3,12, *RSV*, emphasis added). When we pray for someone, we are channeling the power of Jesus Christ to, in and through him or her. While the actual results of this kind of prayer are never predictable, it is always restorative.

In the early chapters of this book, I stated that no one knows what life is. This extraordinary activating energy of existence defies our grasp, but Scripture tells us that Jesus Christ was and is the embodiment of life. Healing ministry is nothing less than conveying His life to the needy. Sometimes it restores bones; sometimes it cleanses the past. His life always gives us the energy we need to continue our journey through this world. Coming to the end of life is not the conclusion of that journey but a preparation for the next leg of the race that happens on the other side. The dying need the same energy when crossing that line, and praying for the dying offers them that energy, that strength. Praying for them as their capacities ebb will continue to bring needed vitality into their lives.

Intercession

Looking further at what happens as we pray, we can find more clues for why intercession is so vital. Most people consider prayer an attempt to make contact with God. They see prayer as a monologue. While they wouldn't say it out loud, they might be thinking that they've got to get His attention or He won't respond to their needs. Prayers are a poke in the divine ribs to get the heavenly Father's eye so that He'll get on the ball and get something done about their current problems. When these folks show up at church, they hope the setting helps the messages get through the sky faster, but it's usually still a monologue. That's the problem.

Prayer was intended to be a dialogue.

At the end of Matthew's Gospel, Jesus vowed that He would be with us always. The risen Lord promised His Church an ongoing connectedness. Relationship is possible only when there is communication that requires two parties to listen and respond. Prayer is both a reaching out *and* a taking in. The receiving is actually more important because we receive life when Christ communicates with us. When we intercede for someone, we also have the opportunity to send this life on to that person.

Here are several illustrations that help me understand how this occurs: A large and powerful electric line runs across the back of our property. The entire neighborhood lights up every night because of the powerful current in these thick lines. However, no matter how strong the electric force is, nothing can happen unless smaller wires direct the flow of electricity into our houses. No connection; no lights.

When people intercede for their relatives and friends in need, they become the human strand that channels power into another person's life just as wire brings electricity into houses. Whether we perceive this fact or not, we are doing something important every time we pray for someone because each time we are genuinely connecting with Jesus Christ.

Consider a magnifying glass. Held at the right angle and distance, the lens can focus the rays of the sun on grass with such intensity that a fire results. The vitality of the sun has been there all the time but it required a human hand to create the proper concentration. God's love is no different. It's around us constantly, but our prayers become like a lens that focuses the power of prayer on a specific human need.

In Genesis 1:28, the Bible tells us about this principle. The passage says that God has given us dominion in this world. The ancient concept of dominion meant that the master, the lord of the estate, gave responsibility to his servants to control a farm and fields. They had absolute control over the land as well as accountability for production. The master waited for his servants to exercise authority and produce fruit. This same idea can be applied to the entire planet. We were created to have authority in this world and our Creator waits for us to extend dominion over the world around us through our actions, intentions and prayers.

Interceding is a part of this responsibility. While most of us think of prayer as optional, in fact it's not optional at all. By praying for those on their deathbeds, we are extending petitions directly to God for His creation. We may have some idea or perceive what is physically happening as a person is dying or we might have no such insight at all. Regardless, I believe that our prayers can offer the support and encouragement the dying need for crossing to the other side.

The mental image that I find most helpful as I intercede for someone is to seek to come into relationship with Jesus Christ through prayer before I see the dying person. I seek to know that I am in a valid and vital contact with the Lord. This kind of preparation might even continue over an extended period of time. Then, as I enter the room, I silently try to keep this contact alive by praying inwardly. Sometimes I will maintain a constant flow of praise or I may pray the following prayer over and over again: "Lord Jesus Christ, Son of God, have mercy on me. Lord Jesus Christ, Son of God, have mercy on this person." I believe that praying in this mode for an extended period of time allows Christ to meet whatever need the person has.

When you attempt to pray in this manner, you may be unaware of anything happening, but the answer is not in you. It's in the risen Lord!

A Hands-on Experience

No one could tickle the imagination like Ruth Eaton. Back in the late '60s, she and her husband, Baxter, were members in the first congregation I led as a pastor. Along the way, their young daughter Lula Belle died and I held her funeral. Her unexpected death proved deeply painful to Ruth and Baxter. Time went by and a decade later, Ruth joined a new church that I founded. By then, Baxter had died and Ruth was in her 80s, but she hadn't slowed down a notch.

With fierce red hair flying in all directions, Ruth was always on the go. Sometime in her mid-80s, Ruth discovered old people. More by accident than design, she wandered into a nursing home and found a world of forgotten people (many of them younger than she). Ruth did not want these people to simply waste away, thinking no one in the world cared about them. She declared that every forgotten elderly person in Oklahoma City would get a Christmas present, even if it took her all year to prepare the gifts. And Ruth Eaton went to work with a passion!

Ruth's home became a storage center for any item that might make a good Christmas gift for someone. Empty boxes were piled up along the walls. She stacked little bottles of perfume or shaving equipment in one of the bedrooms until they were wrapped with Christmas paper. Whenever there was a sale,

Ruth stood in line to grab whatever items she could find at the lowest possible price for her friends in the nursing homes. Church members pitched in and helped with extra funding to cover the growing expense. She always had access to my office because her ministry was important to me and to our church.

At our church's annual Thanksgiving service, I asked Ruth to remind people that Christmas was coming soon and that she needed their help. I never knew what she'd say but it was always colorful. One Thanksgiving stands out in my memory.

With her red hair graying slightly, Ruth stood behind the pulpit and explained the needs she'd found in various nursing homes around the city. This year, she was particularly concerned for elderly men's gifts.

"You'd be surprised at what they don't have," Ruth explained. "Basic needs aren't met when there's no family." She looked around the congregation at the plump men sitting in the pews. "When I see some of you fat boys, I know you can help me. I want your underwear!"

That was Ruth.

On one particular Friday morning, I told my secretary to hold all the calls, as I had to complete my sermon. Thirty minutes had passed when I heard a commotion in the secretary's office. I listened more intently to pick up what was happening.

"Robert said that he can't be disturbed," the secretary said.

"I don't care!" The voice of Ruth Eaton slipped under the door. "I must see him *now*."

"But," the secretary protested, "you can't . . ."

The doorknob turned on my door and in came Ruth. "I've got to talk to you this instant!" she demanded. "Just can't wait." Her red hair stood out like she'd just gotten her hands on a live wire.

"Right now!"

Ruth plopped down on my couch and launched into her story. She had been at home working on the Christmas presents when it happened. She was sitting on the long divan wrapping boxes in Christmas paper when she started thinking about her daughter who had died years earlier. Lula Belle's life had certainly been cut short and Ruth always felt it was horribly unfortunate. She hoped her daughter was well and felt sure she was in heaven. Then Ruth began to think about her mother. Lula Belle had always favored Ruth's mother so much. As Ruth thought about her mother, she had the funniest feeling that somebody was watching her.

"I looked down at the other end of the couch," Ruth's voice began to shake. "Just seemed like somebody had come in." She stopped and gently tapped her chest. "There they were! Standing there! Lula Belle and my mother."

I stared, not sure that I heard her right.

"They both looked like they were about 25. Didn't look like grandmother and grandchild! They looked so much like sisters that I couldn't believe it. Looked just alike."

"You . . . you're sure you saw them?"

"As real as I'm looking at you," Ruth said, tears filling her eyes. "I couldn't say anything but somehow we began to communicate in our minds. Our words went back and forth like sending thoughts." Ruth reached out and clutched my hand. "They told me that they're having a wonderful time in heaven. Happiness is everywhere and they're waiting for me to come.

It won't be long they said and I can join them."

I had known Ruth for years and never known her not to tell the truth. She had always been of more than sound mind and Ruth always had a vital, truthful and exuberant spirit. There was no question that this experience had touched her profoundly, but how it happened, well, who knows? Ruth Eaton had seen her mother and daughter standing in her living room many years after their deaths. Little did I know, but I would be beside Ruth when she died a few years later. Through this experience and others, I learned some key lessons about how to be with someone during the last weeks, days, hours or minutes of his or her life.

How Can We Help?

One day I was on a prayer retreat, two states away from our church. The leader called me out of the meeting because Ruth Eaton was on the phone asking for me. Reluctantly, he said the old lady wouldn't take no for an answer. Knowing Ruth, I understood his problem! Ruth had called to say the doctor had found cancer and that she wanted me to pray and find out if she was supposed to die.

"Ruth," I told her on the phone, "I can't tell you something like that."

"Yes, you can! You get back in there and do some more prayin'! I want to know what I should get ready for. Call me back as soon as you know."

After an extended prayer time, I had a sense of what I thought was ahead but, of course, I didn't know. When I called Ruth back, I held back everything I had to say to her but she was relentless.

"Come on!" Ruth demanded. "Quit pussy-footing around with me. Tell me what you think."

Finally, I came out with it. "I think there's a strong possibility that your time has come."

"I knew it!" Ruth said. "I knew it. Now, you get that meeting wrapped up and get back here so we can finish this off."

Most people aren't as self-confident as Ruth Eaton. By this time she was in her early 90s. When I returned, she was in the hospital and eager to get on with her death. All she wanted me to do was pray with her and "get things wrapped up."

Through this and other experiences, I have discovered some specific methods that proved particularly helpful to the dying. These simple steps are a form of the same restorative healing that Jesus commanded His followers to do. I believe anyone can make a significant difference with this approach.

Let's remember that Jesus said, "I am the Way, the truth, and the life" (John 14:6). This pronouncement came in His final Upper Room discourse during the Last Supper. The Passover Feast had always been the central religious event for the Jews. During this supper, Jesus both affirmed its meaning and transformed the service. As we stand back and survey this Upper Room scene, we find that Jesus of Nazareth was also performing a highly significant procedure in preparation for His crucifixion. Not only was He teaching His apostles, but Jesus was also helping them see that He was the embodiment of all He had proclaimed. Jesus of Nazareth demonstrated that He was the Christ, the Savior of the world. In this Upper Room discussion, Jesus was not only telling them about a way and a truth that was to come, but Jesus also manifested that He was the personification of these vital ingredients for hope and assurance. He was personally the way into eternity. Jesus was, is and will always be *life*!

As people like Ruth Eaton are dying, they are not only leaving this world behind but they are also entering into a transformation that will actually give them more life than they have ever had before. This perspective helps us understand more completely what Jesus meant when He taught, "I am life!" Therefore, coming into relationship with Jesus Christ is not an abstract idea or a statement of conviction; in fact, when someone dies this relationship becomes a tangible reality. Recognizing this fact gives us a deeper understanding of how we can help people as they die. When Ruth Eaton called on me to come to her hospital bed to "get things wrapped up," in her own unique way she was asking me to pray that the life of Jesus Christ would help her cross that final dividing line. Just as with intercession, we can help dying people by entering into a dialogue with Christ before we arrive in their rooms. When we start praying for them, in some mysterious way we can actually convey some measure of the life of Christ to them.

Steps into Eternity

Here are some simple suggestions for how this can be done. Before I went to Ruth's room, I prepared myself for the encounter in several ways, as I've found that preparation is a vital ingredient in helping during the final hours. Here are some of the ways that might be of help for you.

1. Retreat

Find a quiet room like a chapel where you will not be disturbed. Sit down and spend a few moments clearing your mind. We live in a busy world filled with loud sounds, distractions and constant interruptions. From the time we get up until we go to bed, we've got a television, a radio or the Internet on (and maybe all running at once) and going full blast. Americans have become such consumers of media that it seems as if we're almost afraid of the quiet. We need solitude if we are going to be prepared for this kind of ministry.

2. Prepare

Take a few breaths and release any tension that has built up in you. Attempt to feel your heart slow down and your muscles relax. Often, I begin with a rhythm in which I let my prayers and my breathing coincide. As I breathe in, I pray, "Come, Holy Spirit." When I breathe out, I pray, "Come, Lord Jesus." I do this for as long as it is necessary to achieve a deep sense of inner peace and quiet. As discussed in the section on intercession, I may pray the Jesus prayer over and over: "Lord Jesus Christ, Son of God, have mercy on me." This repetition takes me to the point where my heart, muscles, mind and spirit feel attuned to God. While this may seem lengthy, I've found that praying for an hour in this manner can be important and helpful later. The task isn't to follow a clock but to walk the inner path to the place where you connect with Jesus Christ. Anyone who has never done this, or something like this, may feel they don't need this kind of lengthy preparation. If you feel that way, perhaps that's a sign that you do need preparation after all!

3. Meditation

Every person has a unique way of discovering how God speaks to him or her. It's different in each of us but we all need to confirm that we're not talking to ourselves and making up what we think Jesus might be telling us. Some years ago, I discovered a small but important clue for me.

Once I was walking into a hospital after receiving a phone call that a parishioner was in serious condition. Without closing my eyes, I prayed, asking God if the person would live. Abruptly, a no leaped into my mind. I literally stopped and leaned against the wall. I prayed the same prayer a second time. Once more the answer came: "No, he will not live." This came as a great surprise because it was completely foreign for me to believe that someone would die. In other instances I have felt God speak in ways that were so foreign that I knew that the thought didn't come from me. Your experience might be quite different but I have found that it's important to have some sense of when the Lord is truly speaking, and what He is saying.

So before I leave this quiet space, I ask for guidance as to what the Lord has in mind for the dying person. Is it possible the person will recover? If not, how long does the person have? What needs to be done? What can I do to be of help? Is there something specific that I personally should do? These and similar questions guide me as I attempt to sort out what my next step should be. Though it doesn't always happen, my goal is to let the Lord speak and to be open to that possibility.

And how does that happen? While I'm careful not to sanctify anything that runs through my head, I find that our thought life is often the place where the Lord can speak most clearly.

When an idea comes to mind, I try to carefully check it out and come to some sense of whether this might be the Lord's direction. Usually, after an extended period of quiet reflection, I begin to develop some sense of what I should do. If I don't, I continue praying for this person. Then I leave this quiet area and go directly to the dying person.

4. Listen

Throughout this book we've emphasized that listening to the dying is more important than giving advice or making any kind of assertions. In addition, we've examined the role that symbolism can sometimes play in what these dying people communicate. I come to the individual with all these possibilities in mind. When I reach the person's room, I try to enter unobtrusively and am quiet until I get a clear reading of the situation. Even if the person is in a coma, don't assume he or she can't hear you. He or she may be quite attuned to what is happening. I've also found that someone with his or her eyes closed may have only decided to tune out distractions in the room but is still awake. At some point, the person may surprise us by opening his or her eyes and communicating with clarity that he or she knows everything that is going on. Never assume any lack of awareness on the person's part or make statements that you wouldn't make if talking directly to him or her.

5. Inform

When the times comes to pray aloud for the person, I tell him or her what I am doing so that as I touch the person and pray out loud, he or she will know what is occurring. It is important that the patient know what is unfolding. In addition, I often give the person some insight about how he or she can pray with me. I might offer a Scripture or a prayer that he or she can pray along with me. Possibly, I'll suggest that the person quietly or inwardly pray, "Yes, Lord," over and over again as I intercede. Because we don't always know exactly where the patient is spiritually, we need to give that person the freedom to do what he or she feels needs to be done. A few words of explanation can help the patient significantly.

6. Ritual

The laying on of hands or anointing with oil has become common with many groups and doesn't require the ordained. Rather than simply following a biblical procedure or ritual, I find these highly important symbols help connect with the life of Christ.

Generally, I begin by anointing the individual by making the sign of the cross on his or her forehead with oil. This is common in many Christian traditions. While I am doing this, I pray a simple prayer out loud saying, "I anoint you with oil in the name of the Father, and of the Son, and of the Holy Spirit. Amen." I may also pray that the Holy Spirit inwardly anoint the person to deliver him or her from all evil and preserve him or her in goodness as well as bring him or her to everlasting life.

If I don't know the person well, I may ask him or her if I can hold his or her hand. That's a fairly impersonal starting point. After praying in this position for a while, I will often tell the person that I wish to lay my hands on his or her forehead or the top of his or her head. Not only is this moving closer, it can prove to be a point of more significant contact. If my prayers are making an important connection, sometimes my hands will become warm or even hot. Many of the people that I have worked with over the years have had this same experience.

7. Acceptance

The dying person may make little or no response as I finish. However, the lack of acknowledgment may mean nothing. As we noted earlier, people may groan or make loud noises during the final hours. This doesn't necessarily mean they are in physical pain but is a good sign that our prayers can help them past this point. In fact, it may require an hour of prayer before they will come through this time and become quieter. Once you've seen someone return to peaceful sleep after your prayers appeared to help him or her, you'll be ready to pray at every opportunity you get!

Conclusion

What does it take to have a ministry that encourages and helps the dying? Courage. Everyone feels reluctance when they consider praying for another person, much less touching that person, and especially if he or she is dying. We all fear that nothing will happen and we'll look like a fool. Just remember to put your faith in God rather than in yourself.

We began this book with a glance at the apostle Paul's promise that faith, hope and love abide but the greatest of these is love. We end the book by remembering that love is caring enough to put the other person's needs above our own. Ultimately, that's what praying for the dying is all about: caring for them as if they will be with us for endless centuries . . . because perhaps they will be!

This book began with the hope that it would help you face death with new confidence and certainty. We have examined the near-death experiences and near-death awareness and found that they resonate with biblical promises. What Jesus Christ promised us in Scripture certainly seems to be realized all around us. At least 15 million people have walked over the line and come back unafraid of death. I find this to be extraordinarily encouraging.

I hope you do too.